May this jour
peace & ha..
life, so you can turn around &
spread it into your world!
Sudeep Brar ——— ⁰

WHAT'S THE POINT OF LIFE, DEATH, AND THE UNIVERSE?

FIND OUT WHY YOU EXIST

403-259-3900

FROM 2nd Hand
Book Store

Gurdeep Brar

Produced by:

FriesenPress

Suite 300 – 852 Fort Street
Victoria, BC, Canada V8W 1H8

www.friesenpress.com

Distributed to the trade by The Ingram Book Company

Spirituality is not something you practice. It is a major part of who you already are—more important than your career, your relationships, your health, and your material possessions.

— Gurdeep Brar

To God:
Thank you for giving me this honor.

To my parents, Amarjit and Sukhdev Dhaliwal:
Thank you for always loving me and encouraging me to follow
my dreams. This book happened because of your support.

To my husband Dampy, my sister Harjeet, and my friend Karen K:
Thank you for going on this journey with me.

To the loves of my life, Saiva and Saachi:
Thank you for choosing me as your mother.

To you:
Thank you for showing up—it is not a coincidence that you are here.
May this book help you find meaning and purpose for your existence.

Contents

INTRODUCTION

Seven billion people live on Earth: a place each one of us calls home. People with different skin colors reside in 195 countries around the world. No two people have the same DNA, and no personalities are identical. No one knows the day a person will be born, and no one can predict the day a person will die. Breathtaking sunrises start our days, and at night, countless stars accompany the moon to light up the dark sky. There are so many wonders in this world; we cannot even begin to count them all.

Human intelligence has developed languages, societies, politics, and economics. Man has created objects such as bridges, dams, satellites, and space shuttles. Science and technology have advanced so much that they have predicted how all this came into existence. Approximately 13.7 billion years ago, a Big Bang occurred in the universe, and through a long complex chain of events, the planet Earth was created. After millions of years of evolution, the human race came to be.

According to scientific discoveries, you and I, along with everything else in this world, simply exist because of a coincidental accident that occurred in the universe billions of years ago. There was no purpose. There was no plan. It just happened. I do not disagree with science or its scientific theories; however, I cannot write off the human experience as a mere coincidence.

I feel, I laugh, and I cry. I experience tremendous love, joy, pain, and agony with every inch of my being. How can all this just be a byproduct of a scientific phenomenon? There has to be more. There has to be a point. I'm sure the Big Bang Theory is accurate, but it did not happen by chance or coincidence. I believe there is no such thing as a coincidence. The Big Bang, like everything else, must have been premeditated. A higher power must have caused it for a very specific reason. Someone or something intricately planned, created, and continues to maintain all that exists. The question is *why*?

This world is an amazing place where children's laughter, beautiful landscapes, and wonderful experiences occur. However, it cannot be denied that an underlying sadness and sorrow exists within the human race. From what I can see, billions of people are lost, confused, scared, and detached. Billions more are simply going through the motions of life, wrapped up in acquiring and maintaining material goods. So many people are in the mental state of what I call *material-comatose*.

Perhaps the human race has been suffering this way for thousands of years, or perhaps this has come to an all-time high in our lifetime. I do not know. I have heard that many studies suggest that we are becoming a more depressed and anxious society with every passing decade. More people are using antidepressants and sedatives than ever before.

Economic inequality, acts of war and terrorism, and poverty have saddened me to my core. In our world, guns, bombs, and nuclear weapons are used to kill, destroy, and conquer. Innocent children are beaten and raped. Genocides and ethnic cleansing happen in the name of God and religion. How can we call ourselves a civilized society? What kind of world has man created? I cannot help but wonder what is missing inside of human nature that allows such things to happen.

Ever since I was a child, I have internalized and felt the pain of others. Whether it's a family member, a friend, someone on the news, or a bug trapped inside my house, my heart goes out to them. I want to do everything in my power to help. However, I have been unable to solve people's true problems, and I was incapable of alleviating pain and suffering. This made me feel powerless, and when you are powerless, compassion becomes an impossible burden to carry.

I have spent years feeling as though, in this gigantic world, I am just one person—one person who has no control. I felt helpless. I even went through phases where I stopped watching the news, but I soon realized that out of sight did not mean out of mind. Even though I was not watching the horrific scenes of people suffering on the news, my feelings of sadness and helplessness did not go away.

As I write this—at this very moment—tears are pouring down my face. My chest feels heavy and my heart is aching. Just a few years ago, I remember being a 32-year-old woman carrying the burden of the world on my shoulders. Every morning I would wake up feeling as though the world's problems were my problems.

I was terrified of my morality, petrified of death, and I was frightened for everyone else whose death was inevitable. I would lie in bed at night and worry that my parents and loved ones must be worried about dying. Having a three-year-old son and being pregnant with my second child amplified these feelings. How was I going to explain this world to my children? How was I going to explain their life and their impending deaths to them? Through the thousands of questions I had, one kept haunting me—*what is the point? What is the point of it all?*

After being completely consumed by fear and confusion, I was compelled to try and do something. I had to help myself. I had to help my family, and I had to do something for my world. It literally made me sick to my stomach to think about how I was going to do this. How was I going to help people who are dealing with turmoil in their lives? How was I going go to change people and motivate them to help make this world a better place? How was I going to help others understand their lives and not be afraid of death? Talk about having high ambitions!

An onion is often used as an analogy for getting to the center of a problem. You need to peel the layers of an onion, one at a time, to get to its core—to get to the truth of something. Metaphorically speaking, I spent years feeling like I was trapped inside the center of a large onion. I had layers and layers of knowledge and understanding around me but I had no means of accessing it.

When religion, self-help books, and other people tried to define the realities of our existence for me, I did not have the capacity to understand them fully. I found a lot of the information to be confusing, too deep, and too philosophical. Often a voice inside told me that these theories and ideas were not quite right. This made me even more confused and fearful.

I was completely lost. So I prayed, and I put my heart-filled intent into the universe. I wanted to learn and understand the greater meaning of our existence. I asked for the non-visible truths of our reality to become clear to me.

Finally, one day I had an epiphany, which most certainly came as an answer to my prayers. I needed to peel the layers of my onion from the inside out—one at a time. I had to start at the core and work my way out. I call this reverse peeling of an onion my spiritual journey.

Through countless realizations and epiphanies that came at an unimaginable speed, I learned, and finally, I understood. I rose to a much higher level of awareness. All the confusion went away and everything started to make sense. I left my sadness and helplessness behind. I freed myself! I comprehended that, to find God and understand His or Her creation, I needed to first find myself and understand the life that I have been creating. It is a journey that absolutely went from the inside out. Surprisingly, I found the answer to my most fundamental question: *what's the point of life, death, and the universe*?

I have been so inspired by author, educator, and global renaissance woman Maya Angelou. She says, "When you get, you should give," and "When you learn, you should teach." I know I have been given an incredible gift, and it is not meant for me alone. The idea of becoming a teacher is incredibly humbling; however, it is undeniable that everything that has happened in my life has led me to this moment. It has led me to write this book. I have always wanted to help people and make a difference in the world; I think this book is my way of starting that process.

Before I talk the talk, I want you to know that I have walked the walk. Externally I have been a fairly successful woman; however, internally my story was completely different. During different periods in my life I have been insecure, depressed, and self-loathing. I have struggled with loss, debt, failure, and many other problems. I have felt unworthy and did not know my purpose in life. I can relate to the many issues you may be going through in your life. Fortunately, I have survived all of these struggles. I came out the other end, feeling worthy, satisfied, peaceful, and happy.

This book will tell you everything that I learned. I will show you what I did to become highly successful on both the inside and the outside. Personally, I do not believe that awareness, self-discovery, and spirituality can be taught. They already exist within you, so they can only be inspired or awoken.

This book is not filled with fancy words of inspiration and motivation. It is not a deeply complicated philosophical book. It is not going to list instructions on how to better your life. It is not generic, and I don't believe it will leave you confused with more questions than when you started. I hope it isn't something that you will read through in a few days and leave behind. How many times have you read a self-help book or gone to a seminar and been inspired? How long did that inspiration last? Did it move you to action? As human beings, we are easily distracted. Often our motivation and drive fades quickly, especially when it comes to working on our internal life.

If the effects of my words are not permanent, then I did not do my job as an author. I designed this book as a course. You will have to use these thoughts and ideas to work through your own life. This book will peel the layers of your onion, one at a time, from the inside out. It will take you on a special journey of your own.

One of my favorite quotes from Albert Einstein is, "If you can't explain it simply, you don't understand it well enough." In the simplest way I know how, I identify and define what our relationship is with the universe, the spirit world, God's realm, and the paranormal world. In detail, I explain what the point of life is, what happens when we die, and where we go in the afterlife. Through anecdotes about my life and my journey, and by providing detailed instructions, I will teach you how to significantly improve every aspect of your life, including relationships, parenting, career, health, and spirituality. I will help you find your worth and your purpose in life. More importantly, I believe each one of us is here to change the world. I will show you exactly what you can do to help heal the world and achieve peace and happiness for all.

I have struggled with how I would provide proof for what I am about to say, but then I realized that I did not need any proof. A voice inside me told me what was right and what was not quite accurate. The things I am about to share with you resonated deep inside of me as the truth. I have made the conscious decision not to confuse my message by backing it with so-called proofs—after all, proof is subjective.

While reading this book there may be many times where you have questions, such as, *How does she know that?* or *Where did that information come from?* The only answer I can give you upfront is that they came from within me. Some revelations came through meditation, some came from my soul and my intuition, and other ideas were built on thought processes that others evoked in me. Also I am currently pregnant. Perhaps some of this is coming from my baby, whose heart is beating inside of me, yet is still one with the creator.

I love the saying, "A skeptic is proven right time and time again." If you go into a situation as a skeptic, you will likely find something to prove your skepticism correct. It is great that you are right; however, what have you learned. If you enter something as a non-believer, you deny yourself the opportunity of learning or experiencing something new. I ask you to please read on with an open mind and let your own intuition guide you. You may be surprised with how much of what I say resonates within you as the truth.

Physically writing things down is an integral part of learning and growing. I'm sure you remember that from school. Simply thinking about things does not allow you to track your progress. Thinking about things does not provide you with a reference guide. You need to write your thoughts down. This book is your working journal, so please go ahead and write in it. Pick up a highlighter and highlight things that intrigue you. Circle thoughts and ideas that resonate with you. I want you to use my words to reflect on your own life.

At the end of most chapters, I will strategically ask you to answer a few short questions. This will help you relate concepts and ideas to your own life. This way you will understand your life. You will be guided to find the meaning and purpose for your existence.

Reflecting on the past is important because past situations and events leave cuts and wounds in our life's story. Even though you have put bandages over them, most of them are likely still bleeding and causing pain. In order to move forward, we need to go back and revisit each wound. As uncomfortable as it may be, we need to momentarily relive our heartbreaks and our heartaches. If you follow my lead, I will help you heal all old wounds, and once and for all, put the past where it belongs—in the past. By answering the questions at the end of each chapter, you will get to know yourself in a way you never thought possible. By answering these questions, you will know where you are, where you have been, and where you are going.

There is a saying, "Your life should be like an open book." You shouldn't have any secrets and you shouldn't hide anything from anyone. By writing this book, my life has actually become an open book. I encourage you to also make this your mantra. Go to www.gurdeepbrar.com and write your answers and your revelations as you go. Also as you're reading this book, post things on facebook and twitter and let your social network in on your journey. It will liberate you and bring you closer to people.

Often our relationships deteriorate because we don't have meaningful things to talk about. Watching movies, eating dinners, and running errands with people do not create solid bonds—communication does. This book is a communication tool. A tool to communicate with yourself and with others. I encourage you to get another copy of this book for your significant other, or for anyone whom you wish to have a deeper connection with. You can read it simultaneously and discuss it. At the end of each chapter, you can share your thoughts and your answers with each other. This way you and your loved ones will have something meaningful to talk about. You will get to know each other on a much deeper level.

Before you continue, take a moment to officially start your journey by answering the following questions. If you need more space there are blank pages in the back. If you are reading electronically, then start a journal and write down your answers in that. It is my sincerest request that you do not skip through this step. There is a reason why you picked up this book. There is a reason why you are here right now reading these very words. You picked up this book to improve your life, so please be actively involved in the process. Don't just skim through the pages. You owe it to yourself to participate and to try. This will help you track the progress you are about to make. Also I will be asking you to come back and revisit your answers.

Don't think about the questions too much; just write down what comes to mind. I know that most answers are not black and white, but I want you to choose yes or no for a specific reason.

1. Yes or No. Have you ever thought about what the point of life is?
   If yes
   a. *Yes* or *No.* Did you find an answer?
   b. In a few words what do you think the point of life is?

   To be as happy as possible

2. *Yes* or No. Have you ever thought about what will happen to you when you die?

3. Yes or *No.* Does this scare you?

4. Yes or No. Are you happy?

   Sometimes i'm happy only when I
   usually
   question why we are here am

   I uneasy

5. Yes or No. Do you spend enough time looking inwards and working on your internal life?

   Maybe too much?

6. Yes or No. Do you consider yourself a spiritual person?

7. After reading the title of this book and the introduction, list two or three questions that come to your mind about this topic?

   - Is this book going to attempt to convert me to a specific religion?

   — Will i follow through?

8. What are you skeptical about?

   — If I will follow through

   — If this will give me peace or mess me up even more

CHAPTER 1: THE ELEPHANT IN THE ROOM

In a discussion about spirituality, it is difficult to ignore religion. No matter how much we try to avoid the subject, it will remain the *elephant in the room*. Before we move on, it needs to be addressed.

Religion has shaped our world from pretty much the beginning of civilization. Various religions around the world have their own theories about how the world was created, who created it, and for what purpose. I have always been fascinated by religion in general, and I have studied most of the world's religions.

My family has a strong faith in God. Sikhism is the religion that I was born into, and it is a religion that I adore and greatly respect. I consider myself a very religious person. However in the past, the trials and tribulations of life have put my faith to the test many times. During different periods of my life, I have gone from being extremely religious, to seriously doubting that a God even exists. I partly blame my confusion on the differences that exist within religions.

The way I see it, when it comes down to fundamental values, all religions basically teach the same things. This is why it baffles me that religion has ultimately split our world apart. Don't you think that religion has done more to separate and isolate the human race than it has done to bring it together?

Jesus, Moses, Confucius, Mohammad, Buddha, Guru Nanak, and the other messengers of God came to earth to enlighten and to unify the world—one God one message. Their teachings were pure, and they had the utmost love for mankind as a whole. Sadly, in a lot of cases, God's true message has been lost. People conveniently pick and choose the messages they wish to live their lives by. People's actions, and their interpretation of religion, have taken religion and made it comparable to politics. In fact, in a lot of countries there is no differentiation between religion and state.

If you break apart history and really think about it, religion has been used to control masses of people and used to isolate others. Historically, each religion has created a group of believers and a group of non-believers. These two groups have then further subdivided amongst themselves— this is why most religions have many sects and divisions. These various groups of people stopped seeing eye-to-eye and stopped communicating with each other. Eventually anger, discrimination, and hatred started to foster—and here we are today.

Every religion was supposed to teach the exact same things. The messengers and messiah's all came from the same source—from the same creator. If they came from the same creator then how could they possibly have different messages? It is human interpretation that has confused the messages. I am not against religion, and I certainly do not mean any disrespect. I am simply against what some people have done with religion.

I truly believe that all of the world's religious bibles and texts are like different currencies—each one holds worth and has its own precious value. It may upset some people to hear this, but like currencies, religious doctrines have also shifted and changed throughout the years. No one can say, without a shadow of doubt, that some things have not been added, and some teachings have not been forgotten or left out. Take a moment to think about that.

I think that most people in the world are now in agreement that there is only one God, or higher power, that created and governs all that exists. Regardless of the name we choose to use, there is only one creator, one power, and one God. However, some people still debate and argue against this notion. They have faith in what they presume is their God and strongly disagree with other religions. Furthermore they preach that others will be condemned in the afterlife for not believing in their God.

Over the years, I have had this conversation with many people who preach their religion. I tell them that I am a Sikh, but it's okay because there is only one God anyways. They usually say, 'Yes the God we believe in is the only God.' I try to explain that we have a different name for God, but again there is only one higher power. To which they answer, 'but your God does not exist. You need to be praying to the God in our religion, otherwise you will not be saved.' Again there is only one God regardless of the name one gives to the divine power—all of the world's religions are referring to the same God. Frankly, this is such a silly religious debate.

You need to ask yourself, is it possible that at least one of your fundamental beliefs is based on a message that was confused or misinterpreted hundreds of years ago? Perhaps something that you absolutely do not believe in was meant to be in your religious doctrines, but it got omitted somehow. Early on most religions believed that the earth was flat, but today we know that this is not true: science has undeniably proved that the earth is round.

In *Conversations with God: an uncommon dialogue*, author Neale Donald Walsch contends that God told him that the only way to move forward is to ask yourself, "What would happen if everything I thought was 'wrong' was actually 'right'? Every great scientist knows about this. When what a scientist does is not working, a scientist sets aside all of the assumptions and starts over. All great discoveries have been made from a willingness, and ability, to not be right."

Half of the world believes in past lives and in reincarnation, and the other half of the world's religions do not. It is a very real possibility that this is one of those messages that was missed or left out. No one knows for sure how accurate the information in religious doctrines is, and no one can prove it either way.

This is why we should not blindly accept things, nor should we blatantly dismiss them. When approached by a concept, idea, or belief, think about it, gage the evidence, and you be the judge. After all, this is your life and your journey. There is a wonderful saying, "In a group, if no one is asking questions, then no one is thinking." Therefore think, ask questions, get involved, and become enlightened. It is due time that we all get on the same page. We owe it to ourselves, and we certainly owe it to the generations to come.

Just because you question something about your religion, or understand a scripture differently, does not mean that you are betraying your religion. Other people have been interpreting God's messages for us for centuries, and because God made us all equal, we all have an equal right to be actively involved in interpreting and understanding what God intends for us to know. In *Mansfield Park,* Jane Austen famously says, "We all have a better guide in ourselves, if we would attend to it, than any other person can be." This is why I turned inwards to seek my own answers. I turned to the purest source I have access to. I turned to myself, to my spirituality, which is my direct connection to the creator.

Spirituality is often equated to religion, but it is not the same thing. There are countless people who do not consider themselves religious, but say that they are extremely spiritual. I did not understand this concept before. Today I get it. There is a difference. Religion is devotion. It is something that you practice. Spirituality is not something that you practice; it is a major part of who you already are.

When I first started my spiritual journey, I was taking every new thought and idea and trying to find its proof within Sikhism. I would take my epiphanies and revelations and then quickly try to define them in a religious context. I would say things like, "That is a Christian belief," or "I think Buddha said that in Buddhism," or "I don't think my religion believes in that."

After months of struggling to understand, I realized that all the religious correlations I was trying to make were confusing me further. My preconceived ideas and beliefs were stopping me from learning and from growing. Once again I was standing in my own way. In order for me to awaken my consciousness, and to get to a higher level of awareness and understanding, I simply had to put my preconceived thoughts and ideas on the shelf and out of the way. I had to check religion at the door in order to continue on my spiritual journey.

I started to seriously consider every new thought, idea, and belief that came my way, regardless of what my religion said or didn't say about the subject. For a while, oddly enough, the more spiritual I became the less religious I was. This scared me at first, but I trusted in the process. Today my religion and my spirituality go hand-in-hand. I have so much more respect for and understanding of my religion. Now I have the knowledge and the capability to balance the two, but it was a process.

Hopefully you have chosen to read this book with the intent of learning something new. It is my humblest wish and prayer that this book takes you on a journey of your own. However, before you take a single step, you need to drop the baggage of preconceived thoughts and ideas that you have been taught and carry with you; otherwise you will discount all that you read. I do not want you to judge all new ideas as true or false until you have had a chance to read the entire book, and until you have had the opportunity to process these ideas on a deeper level. All of the connections need to be made clear before the entire concept makes any sense.

Whether you are religious or an atheist, take a deep breath and clear your inner slate. Have an open mind, and again allow your inner voice to guide you. Until you can hear your inner-voice, just surrender and trust in the process. Before you know it, your intuition will take over and take you on your own very special, very personal spiritual journey.

Before I proceed, I would also like to clarify one more thing. The human race has given many names in many different languages to the divine creator. All of these names are correct and represent the exact same thing. Because the English name for the creator is God, and because this is an English book, I will use the term God when speaking about the supreme power that guides all that exists. Please keep in mind that, in the context of this book, the term God does not correlate or represent any religion. It is also not attached to any gender—God is neither male nor female, and can be described as both masculine and feminine.

Before proceeding please actively participate in your journey and answer the questions below. I assure you it will be well worth your time in the end.

1. (Yes) or No. Do you believe in a higher power or a divine creator?

2. Yes or No. Are you religious?

    If yes   kind of
    a. What religion do you follow?
    b. Do you consider yourself a preacher of your own religion or a
        person who is open to other people's religious beliefs?

    Catholic, since I was born into it

3. List three fundamental religious beliefs that you agree with?
    - We all have a purpose and things happen for a reason
    - we are all created equal, its what we do later that defines us
    - Everyone is inherently good (Babies) its society that corrupts us.

4. List three fundamental beliefs that you were taught, but over the
    years you have questioned?
    - You should not be selfish and take only take care of yourself
    - Religion is important
    - education = success

5. Yes or No. Do you agree that preconceived ideas and beliefs can
    hinder your ability to learn and grow?

6. Yes or No. Are you willing to clear your slate and temporarily put
    your preconceived ideas and beliefs aside so you can embark on
    this journey?

CHAPTER 2: MIND, BODY AND SOUL

Taking care of your mind, body, and soul has become a popular modern phrase, but what does it mean exactly? Self-discovery, self-awareness, knowing who you are, connecting with your consciousness, and listening to your soul are some very loaded topics that therapists, self-help books, and spiritual teachers often talk about. However, what in the world do these words really mean? They are broad general concepts that can often be confusing. I know they once were for me, so let's break it down and try to clarify them.

BODY:

Let's begin with what we can see. As humans we have a much easier time accepting things that can be seen or touched. We all have a physical form that is visible. Our body is our strongest reality. Regardless of the countless differences among us, we all basically have a functioning body that allows us to work, go places, and experience life.

It is crucial for us to take care of our body in order for it to function efficiently. We need to feed it properly; we have to dispense its waste; we have to wash and clean it, and we need to keep it active. We have all seen and understand the catastrophic results of not properly taking care of a body. Both obesity and anorexia are becoming pandemic illnesses in our generation. Chronic diseases are also on the rise.

Medical research has provided us with a clear visual of what our body's anatomy looks like on the inside. Underneath our skin are muscles, veins, and bones. Further inside the body are organs with various functions, and inside our head is a very complex organ called the brain. The brain is basically the body's command central and its capacity is unfathomable. It is able to process 30 billion bits of information per second.

The human nervous system contains around 28 billion neurons, which are nerve cells designed to create impulses. In total the adult body has nearly a 100 trillion cells. The cell is the basic functional unit of life. When our body completely shuts down, we die, and our human experience ends.

MIND:

The human body would never experience life as we know it if it weren't for our thoughts, our emotions, and our memories. Although we cannot see our mind, today there is little debate on whether or not a mind exists within each one of us. There is, however, debate on what the mind's functions are. Again we cannot see it, nor can we visualize the mind, so humans are unable to fully understand its power and its limitations.

Basically, the mind is responsible for our ability to think, be intelligent, and have rational or irrational thoughts. It is in charge of our creativity, visualizations, and imagination. The mind creates feelings and emotions. It also allows us to store, retain, and remember information and our experiences—which are defined as our memories.

What makes life so interesting is that our mind is private and 100% confidential. We can see other people's physical actions and hear what they choose to communicate with us; however, no one has the slightest idea of what is going on inside someone else's mind. We do not even have full control over our own mind. It is impossible to fully govern it. Often the mind does and thinks whatever it wants. Our body goes to sleep, but the mind keeps thinking. This is a spectacular twist in the human experience.

The mind is also credited with managing the brain's functions. Our mind thinks, *I want to get up and walk across the room*, and simultaneously the brain understands the command and signals the legs to start walking. Our body physically moves and experiences things with very little effort. Therefore, scientifically speaking, the mind controls the body.

The mind and the body work in conjunction to create the human experience, but have you ever thought that there may be a third element in play? As we work, talk, or even read there is a conversation going on inside of us 24 hours a day. No matter how much we distract ourselves, someone or something inside of us keeps talking and talking and talking. Have you ever questioned who is talking, or better put who you are talking to?

Have you ever gotten into your car and then driven through lots of traffic, taken tons of turns and exits, and when you reach your destination you think, *How did I get here? I was not paying attention at all.* Your mind and body paid attention and got you from point A to point B, but that means you were focusing on something other than your mind. Similarly have you ever read a story to a child—and while your eyes are reading, your mind is processing, and your voice is speaking the words—you are not paying any attention to what you are doing? Think about it. How is it possible for you to read, process, and speak without being actively involved and paying attention? How can you split your consciousness away from what your mind and your body are doing? What inside of you is distracting your attention?

Have you ever had a gut feeling about something, but then your mind contradicts that gut feeling? Where do you think that initial gut feeling came from? Have you ever had a negative thought, almost instantly something inside of you says something like, *That's not nice or Don't do that*? Who is holding you to these moral standards?

Have you ever experienced a time when you were upset and you broke down and cried? You cried and cried and cried, and then finally heard a voice deep down inside that told you something like, *Don't worry, you are going to be okay, or pick yourself up and move forward.* I have, and I know it was not a thought created by my mind.

SOUL:

Last year I went to see Dr. Deepak Chopra speak. Dr. Chopra is a medical physician, a scientist, the author of more than 57 books, and a spiritual teacher. In his lecture *Reinventing the Body, Resurrecting the Soul,* which is also the title of his best selling book, he said something that was so profound that it shook me to my core. I thought that science and religion were two separate institutions that would never see eye to eye, but it seems this is no longer the case.

Dr. Chopra talked about numerous things, but one story really stood out to me. For accuracy purposes, I read through a few of his books so I could share the exact story with you. Unfortunately I did not find the story in writing; however, I want to share what I heard. Ultimately the moral of the story is far more important then the exact details.

He told us a true story about a researcher, whose name I have unfortunately forgotten. He was a brain surgeon who, like most doctors, believed that the brain controls the body's physical movements. Since brain surgeries are conducted while the patient is awake, the doctor is able to communicate and talk to the patient during the procedure. During one particular surgery, this doctor manipulated a man's brain and sent his body the signal to raise his arm. After he sent the signal from the brain, the man obviously raised his arm.

The doctor had a profound thought: he asked the man lying on the operation table, "Are you raising your arm?" Now if the brain is the command center for the body, the man should not be able to differentiate where the command came from. The man answered, "No, I am not lifting my arm; you are lifting it for me." The doctor was surprised that this man was able to understand that his free will did not initiate his arm's movement.

The doctor had another idea. He said to the patient, "I am going to send your body the signal to raise your arm and you try to stop it." Now scientifically speaking this should be impossible. The body absolutely has to follow the brain's commands, and in that moment the doctor is controlling the brain. So the doctor sent the signal, and as the arm started to lift upwards, the patient managed to pull his arm to the side. He disobeyed his brain's instruction. The doctor was shocked. He started to think,

"What is it inside the human body that has the capability to override the brain's commands?"

The doctor then spent years researching this idea. During another brain surgery, the doctor was manipulating a female patient's mind. He was recalling memories and smells from the woman's past. He brought to surface a memory she once experienced at the beach. During the surgery, he asked her, "What do you see?" I believe she answered that she was at the beach with her husband and her children. She could smell the salt in the ocean and could feel the heat from the sun. Everything that this woman was seeing and feeling should technically be her reality at the time. The doctor then asked her, "Are you physically at the beach right now?" Astonishingly she said, "No I am on the operating table." Something inside of her was able to interpret that the mind's reality was not indeed her physical reality.

In this manner, the doctor was able to provide scientific evidence to suggest the existence of something other than the mind inside each human being. The most popular term used for this third entity is the soul. I was absolutely flabbergasted—scientists agree that we have a soul? There is some scientific evidence that proves what many religions have been saying for centuries? Yes there is!

I had heard many times before—through various sources—that our souls are very large, and only a small portion of our soul exists within our body. I thought this was a far off idea, but then to hear Dr. Deepak Chopra, a person who comes from a science background, talk about this same idea really got me thinking.

Now when hundreds of people are listening to a lecturer, each person interprets things differently. Each person processes what is being said on his or her own level. Sitting in that auditorium, this is how I interpreted what Dr. Chopra was saying: he said that our bodies live in the realm of time and space. In contrast to our bodies, our soul is extremely large.

Dr. Chopra's next statement is very profound, and it is a notion that may take some time to fully understand. He said, "My soul is not in my body;

my body is in my soul." He said that your body occupies a small portion of your soul. He explained that the rest of your soul lives outside the realm of time and space. In closing he said that science's next phase is to study what exists beyond time and space.

As I listened to these words, I sat in my chair like a deer in the headlights. Afterwards, I wanted to discuss it with people out in the lobby, but apparently everyone I spoke to did not hear this or didn't understand it. Some people said they must have missed that point. I left thinking, *was I the only one who understood the gravity of this idea*? I already believed in the existence of a soul, and I thought I understood it pretty well, but this created a whole new slew of questions.

After that day, I spent a lot of time internalizing this very complex theory. I felt like this was a major key in better understanding myself, and to understanding the human experience. I talked about this with anyone who would listen. I started to study and learn as much about the soul as I possibly could. At the end of all my soul searching (pun intended) I gathered a lot of information and came to my own conclusions.

Finally this is what resonates within me as the truth. Because the soul is directly related to spirituality, I will talk about it in great detail throughout this book. The simplest way I can start to define the soul is:

1. Every single living being has a soul.

2. It is the inner most part of you.

3. The soul is pure, wise, and honest. It is a direct subdivision of God. Like an umbilical cord, it connects us to the divine creator and to all that has been created.

4. The mind, body, and the soul are all completely different entities that unite to create the human experience.

5.   Most philosophers believe that the consciousness is part of the mind. By consciousness I mean your awareness, your sense of self-hood, your free will, and your intuition. I believe that your true consciousness is actually a part of your soul, not your mind.

6.   Our souls are very large. The soul is obviously non-physical; however, the soul's size can be visualized as being so large that it can fill an entire home or a building. Some souls are larger than others.

7.   In relation to the soul, human bodies are very small. It is impossible to fit an entire soul into a body. Imagine for a moment that a large swimming pool full of water represents your soul. Now imagine that a drinking glass is your human body. Can you place all the water from the swimming pool into a drinking glass? Of course not. If you want the two to merge, then the drinking glass (your body) will have to sit inside the swimming pool (your soul). Thus the soul and the physical body can only be connected if the body goes into the soul. Therefore, the soul of a person does not reside inside of his or her body. Rather, because the soul is so large, it is your body that sits inside of your soul!

8.   The body lives within the realm of time and space. This makes sense because, in our world, time passes through days, weeks, and years. We live in a surrounding that is defined by the space around us. After a person dies, time and space is no longer a factor.

9.   The majority of our soul, which is not occupied by our body, lives outside the realm of time and space. If it helps to attach a percentage to this concept, then I would say that 98% of our soul lives outside of our body and only 2% of our soul is attached to our body.

10. Our souls carry every single answer to every single question we may have. 98% of each person has infinite knowledge, wisdom, and understanding. Unfortunately, most people are not even connected to the 2% of the soul, which exists inside of them.

11. I think that the realm outside of time and space is called the spirit world. This is a place where everything occurs under the divine creator's direct orders and supervision. God's helpers and everyone who has died and left our planet reside there.

12. 2% of our soul lives on earth in our human body, and 98% of our soul lives in spirit form in the spirit world.

13. All of the souls, of everything that lives and breathes in this world, are connected on a level that far exceeds our physical human interaction. I believe we are all one-soul family.

14. There is no way that a mother can fit a soul into her womb. Therefore, the soul enters a body as soon as a baby takes his or her first breath.

15. The mind, body, and soul connection is broken when a person's heart stops beating. The mind and the soul exit the body when a person dies. The mind, like a movie camera, records your entire life's experience, and it follows your soul into the afterlife.

16. It is not the body that holds the essence of who you are. Your soul represents who you truly are.

17. We are made up of energy, and as Einstein proved, energy never dies. Therefore, the soul never dies. It simply changes form and lives on. Our souls live on—which means we live on.

Rest assured I will discuss all of these points in much more detail later on in this book. I simply want you to start thinking about these ideas. They will become clear as we proceed forward.

MIND + SOUL + BODY = HARMONY

Mind, body, and soul are fundamental aspects of our existence. They are like pieces of a puzzle. They need each other, and they must work in conjunction with each other to create the complete picture of human existence. The soul is the wise guide which leads us through life. It is the source of where every intention and action begins. The mind is where thoughts and emotions are created and memories are held. The body carries out our intentions and our emotions, and it moves us through life's experiences.

The ideal situation in every human being is to have the soul take charge. The soul decides who you are, what you want, and what you should do. In every given moment, the soul should decide how to react and how to feel. The mind's job is to then create the corresponding thoughts and emotions, and pass them along to the body. The body then carries out the appropriate actions.

When the mind, body, and soul work together in this manner, it creates peace and harmony in one's life. However, when this mind, body, and soul relationship is altered, it creates great dysfunction in one's life.

MIND VS. SOUL

Now going back to my analogy of the onion and peeling the layers from the inside out, let's focus only on the portion of the soul that is directly attached to, or is occupied by, our body.

Again when it comes to the human experience, our mind, body, and soul all work in conjunction with each other. So why did the divine power create a soul and a mind as separate entities? I have spent a lot of time trying to understand this very important aspect of creation.

To understand this I have gone back to the beginning of human life. Babies and children are deeply connected to their souls. Their minds and their souls are in perfect harmony. It is their soul that guides their thoughts and actions. This is why children are so pure, honest, loving, and innocent.

I strongly believe that anger, hatred, jealousy, greed, worry, and fear are all emotions that are taught to us. We are not innately born with them. I know that many people believe that we are born out of sin, and this is why we are predestined to sin and have negative thoughts. With all due respect, this cannot possibly be the case. The word *sin* is defined as an act that violates God's will. We came from God and we are born under God's will, so how can we possibly be born out of sin. I think this religious message has been confused and misinterpreted throughout history. It may have been meant figuratively, and it may have gotten interpreted literally. I am not sure.

What I do know is that each soul is a direct extension of the divine creator, or a subdivision of God. We are one in the same. God has placed a small portion of Him or Herself in each living being. We each carry a small part of the divine light or energy within us. God is pure and incapable of negative intentions and actions; therefore, our souls are incapable of them also.

Sentiments such as animosity, envy, resentment, and selfishness are all taught to us. They are thoughts and emotions created and driven by the mind. The more attention our family and society gives to negative thoughts and behaviors, the more independent and powerful the mind becomes. By allowing the naïve and temperamental mind to take control, we inadvertently weaken the soul's voice.

Eventually the mind and the soul break apart and become two completely independent entities. They become two detached units that no longer communicate with each other. They stop guiding and assisting one another. They no longer exist in peace and harmony. Instead they constantly battle and clash. I think it is this imbalance and internal conflict that causes confusion, isolation, fear, and lack of awareness. Simply put, I would say this is the root cause of human suffering.

We can't always blame our problems on others. So many people get in their own way. They get in the way of their own happiness. They stop themselves from fulfilling their dreams, and they sabotage their own relationships. If you are a person who often gets in his or her own way, now is the time to recognize it. Recognize that your mind is getting in the way of your soul. You are struggling as two different people. You are battling against yourself. I know I have spent years doing this.

There is a beautiful story that really explains this internal struggle. The story is about an Aboriginal grandfather who sits down to talk to his grandson one day. He tells his grandson that inside each one of us there are two animals: two wolves that live and breathe inside of us all. One wolf is kind, humble, compassionate, and loving. The other wolf is ruthless, angry, vindictive, and pessimistic. These two wolves are constantly fighting and battling one another. The grandson then asks his grandfather, "Which wolf wins?" The grandfather answers, "The one that you feed."

I think one wolf in this story represents the mind, and the other wolf is the soul. I want to be clear that I am not saying that the mind is an evil or negative entity; however, if it is not controlled and managed properly, it does have the potential to become that way. It can take over and destroy your life in many ways. This is a lesson that can be applied to each one of us. Which wolf have you been feeding? Which wolf has been winning inside of you?

MIND – SOUL = EGO

Neurologist Sigmund Freud, who is the founding father of psychoanalysis, created a structural model of the psyche, which he called the psychic apparatus. In *An Outline of Psychoanalysis (1940)*, Freud assumes that "mental life is the function of an apparatus to which we ascribe the characteristics of being extended in space and of being made up of several portions (Id, ego, and super-ego)." According to this model of the mind, the

id is the set of uncoordinated instinctual trends; the ego is the organized,
realistic part: and the super-ego plays the critical and moralizing role.

Many of us may remember first hearing the word ego from Sigmund Freud's theory in school, and this is why I bring it up. However, the word *ego* has a very different spiritual meaning also. Eckhart Tolle, in *The Power of Now*, says that "it means a false self, created by the unconscious identification with mind." I'd like to break this down and simplify it.

Ego is a Latin word which means "I". In English we usually associate the word *I* with *self* or *identity*. Therefore the ego is an identification of one's self. So you may be asking, *What's wrong with that?* Well from a spiritual perspective, to have an ego means that you consider yourself to be distinct from others and from God. The ego is a false sense of selfhood. Without exception, every spiritual teacher says we must transcend the ego to fully know one's self.

In *Beyond the Frontier of the Mind*, Osho says that, "The ego is an accumulated phenomenon, a by-product of living with others." He says that the ego is a social by-product, which creates a social need. I think that the ego is created when the mind and the soul are disconnected. The soul is supposed to communicate intentions and sentiments to the mind. The mind then creates the corresponding feelings and emotions. Again children are deeply rooted into their souls. They do not have egos. When we get older, we start internalizing other people's thoughts and actions, so yes society plays a major role in distracting us from our souls.

Eventually when the sacred bond between the mind and the soul is broken, the mind becomes independent. The independent mind still needs to take lead from something. The mind is not a leader; it is a follower. It has to follow the guidance of another entity. Therefore, when the soul no longer fills that role, the mind creates an ego entity. It creates a false self-image of one's self. Instead of listening to the soul, the mind then starts to listen to the ego. Therefore, the soul is your true self and the ego is your false self.

Simply put the ego is everything that the soul is not. The ego is naïve. It is an illusion created by the mind, so it has no clue about who you are. It constantly creates unrealistic expectations for what you should be. It constantly tells you to do things, and keeps changing course. This is why you are often confused.

The ego is egotistical. It turns a gentle understanding person into a selfish, self-centered person. You may not consider yourself a conceited person, but I am sure at some point you have been a defensive person. When someone says something slightly negative to us, we instantly feel offended. We take people's words out of context and get sensitive. We feel like they are insulting us or attacking us somehow, even if this is not their intention. Some people react by attacking back, and others react by feeling hurt and sad. Think about it, What are you defending? Why are you so sensitive? This is an irrational way to relate to people, which is driven by your ego.

The soul guides the mind through love, whereas the ego guides the mind through fear. The reason why the ego has such a strangle hold on most people is because it leads with fear. It creates fear within people and keeps them distracted from living in the present moment. Fear constantly makes people think about the past or the future.

I believe that once the mind has creates an ego, there is no turning back. You cannot completely destroy the ego. The only thing you can do is be aware of its existence, and try to control it. The way you control your ego is by not following its commands. You will separate the ego from the mind by reconnecting with your soul. You will weaken the voice of your ego when you strengthen the voice of your soul.

All of us has an ego in our mind. For simplicity sake, I will refer to the mind and the ego as one in the same. Going forward, I will discuss the mind with the assumption that you understand that the mind I speak about is driven by the ego.

I believe that self-discovery, self-awareness, knowing who you are, connecting with your consciousness, all these things basically mean reflecting and understanding your relationship between your mind, body, and soul. Before you can fathom changing your life, you need to fully understand what you have been dealing with internally thus far. It is a slow process that begins at the surface, and slowly but surely, we will get to its core.

Start thinking about your mind, body, and soul relationship by answering the following questions. It is imperative that you answer these questions before proceeding. They are tough questions, and I understand the answers are not black and white. However, I do want you to pick either yes or no for a specific reason. If you simply cannot answer, then write down, "I don't know." As you proceed, you will get to know yourself on a deeper level. You can then come back and answer the question.

Yes or No. Do you think your mind, body, and soul are in harmony?

1. Yes or No. Do you have body issues? Are you self-conscious of your body? My Skin, Muscle

2. Yes or No. Do you take good care of your body?

3. Yes or No. Do you believe in a soul?

4. Yes or No. Do you think that your mind and soul are disconnected?

5. Yes or No. Do you believe that your mind has created an ego?

6. Yes or No. Do you have ego driven thoughts?

7. Yes or No. Do you react to your ego driven thoughts?

8. Yes or No. Are you a person who often compliments others?

9. Yes or No. Is it easy for you to accept a compliment?

10. Yes or No. Are you good at teaching people things?

Depends what

11. Yes or No. Is it easy for the people in your life to teach you things?

Also depends

12. Yes or No. Does other people's success make you feel genuinely happy?

If no

a. Does other people's success make you feel inadequate?

Yes

13. Yes or No. Are you angry with others?

If yes

a. Who are you angry with?

I am angry only when I See certain people.

ex

b. Why are you angry with these people?

They are a symbol of my stupidity

14. Yes or No. Are you angry with yourself?

If yes

a. Why are you angry with yourself?

I am not accomplishing enough and reaching My potential

15. (Yes) or No. Do you often get hurt or offended?

If yes *Depends who its from*

a. Why do you think you are so sensitive? What made you this way?

I am self concious about alot of things

16. (Yes) or No. Are you a defensive person?

If yes

a. Why are you so defensive? What made you this way?

I believe my ways are correct most of the tim

17. (Yes) or No. Are you a jealous person?

If yes

a. Who are you jealous of?

W.J, D.T, Y.M, AP,

18. We are all envious of someone. Who are you envious of and why?

W.J due to his work ethic and grades

19. (Yes) or No. Do you love yourself?

If no

a. Have you ever loved yourself?

20. For the past few years have you been feeding the positive wolf inside of yourself or the negative wolf?

Mostly the positive one.

CHAPTER 3: MATERIAL-COMATOSE

Before you read this chapter, please answer the questions below. Again please do not skip through this step, for it will hinder your learning process. I will be asking you to come and review these answers at a later point.

1. List your daily routine from the moment you wake up to the moment you go to sleep on a typical day:

   —Shower
   — eat breakfast / wear clothes
   — Drive to school
   ‐ Go to classes
   ‐ Study
   — workout
   — browse the web
   — eat
   ‐ hangout with friends
   — waste time
   — Dinner
   — ready for bed

2. List your possessions that you are you most proud of:

   — car   — laptops
   —clothes   — phone

3. Go through your above list and write down why each possession is important to you and how it makes your feel?

Car- Gets me to where I need to be

Clothes- Shows who I am

Phone- Keeps me connected

laptop

4. List the possessions you wish you had:
-phone accorries
- Juicer
- skin treatment stuff
- more clothes

5. How does not having these make you feel?

- like I am not becoming the bes

Every day most of us wake up in the morning with a large to-do list. We rush off to get to work, either in the home or in the office. After a long exhausting day of work, we get some errands done, have dinner, and prepare for the next day. If we are lucky, we squeeze in some time to spend with our loved ones, and/or have some fun.

As a society we are completely wrapped up in wanting, obtaining and maintaining our homes, our belonging, our jobs, and our money. All these things are material goods—worldly possessions. The majority of us are incapable of seeing past the physical things that exist in this world. We often forget that the material things we spend our entire lives acquiring all get left behind when we die.

The word *comatose* is defined as being in a state of deep unconsciousness for a prolonged or indefinite period of time. This is usually the result of a severe injury or illness. I think that the human race is predominantly in a severe state of what I call *material-comatose*. If we are disconnected from our soul, where our consciousness resides, then we are in a state of deep unconsciousness. We have severely injured ourselves by slicing the sacred bond that connects our mind and our soul. This tunnel vision, in which we are trapped, is more dangerous and more harmful than any illness in the world. This state of *material-comatose* causes stress, tension, and depression.

Obviously we all have basic needs that have to be fulfilled. We need food, water, and a safe shelter in order to keep our bodies functioning and alive. However, let's face it, there are a lot more things that our mind wants and stresses over. Nobody wants to feel anxious or overwhelmed, so we do everything in our power to put our mind at ease. We say things to ourselves such as:

When I move into a bigger house or apartment, I will feel better.

I need to buy a new car, so I can stop stressing.

When I get this renovation project done, I will stop worrying.

If I make more money than my friend, I will have more confidence.

Buying new clothes will give me higher self-esteem.

When I get a new job, I will have peace of mind.

Being in a state of *material-comatose* does not necessarily mean that you are a materialistic person. To different degrees, we all like to have nice things, and yes, all the material creations of our civilization are wonderful perks of being human. However, we need to assess what these material things really mean to us. What do they really give us? Does money and worldly possessions give you self-worth, self-respect, adrenaline, dignity, confidence, power, or something else?

Attaching emotions and feelings to worldly possession is very risky. If you think that your job and your income defines your self-worth and your confidence, the loss of that job—or a pay cut—threatens your self-worth and security. If shopping and buying new things gives you an adrenaline rush and makes you feel powerful, and you can no longer afford such luxuries, then you lose the excitement in your life. You may start to feel powerless. In this manner, not only do you lose material things, but you also lose a part of yourself emotionally.

You cannot correlate your financial worth to your self-worth. These worldly ups and downs in life create too many internal problems and too much emotional turmoil. People often say that money is not everything in life, but money gives you freedom. Money equals freedom; it is such a popular belief that Lotto 649 has created a great advertising campaign around this notion. Yes, money can buy you the freedom to go places and experience things physically; however, it cannot help you feel free on the inside. You can be completely free and rich on the outside, yet feel completely trapped and emotionally bankrupt on the inside.

If you think about it, we seek material things to calm our minds and to make ourselves feel better on the inside. There is a fundamental problem with doing so—your mind is not a material or a physical entity, and physical things cannot satisfy it. It's like giving an injured and dehydrated rescue animal some clothes, some money, and a fancy new car and expecting that these things will save its life. That would be absurd. The two things have nothing to do with each other. Well this is the kind of logic us humans are using.

Let me put it this way, when your hands get dirty, you wash them with water. When your clothes get filthy, you wash them with soap. When your mind is soiled with negativity, destructive, or pessimistic thoughts and emotions, how can material possessions be a solvent to clean it? They cannot. Physical and material things cannot make you feel better on the inside. Your mind can only be cleansed by spirituality and by reconnecting with your soul.

I want to talk a little bit about the financial crisis of 2007- 2009, which is still impacting the global economy today. Many of us blame the economic crash on government oversights and poor regulations. It is blamed on financial institutions for exploiting people by giving them loans that they didn't have the capability to repay.

Historically there have been many ups and downs in the economy, but this crisis is unlike the world has ever seen before. In *Temptation: Finding Self-Control in an Age of Excess*, Daniel Akst calls this the people's crash. He states that people's lack of self-regulation is the major reason the world is in such dire economic dismay. Akst says that nearly all of us took part in this crisis because of "our swollen homes and credit card balances, our $4 coffees and gas-guzzling SUVs on lease." He adds that reckless spending and risky investments were once limited to the rich, and now it is a course open to practically everyone.

Akst believes that our appetites have evolved because the space for indulging them has expanded. Countless experiments have shown that we often don't know why we do things. He says that "Behaviorism suggests that we are merely creaking robots responding to environmental inputs." I think the reason we are over spending and under saving is again because we are in a state of *material-comatose*. We are trying to buy our way to peace and happiness. We are not regulating ourselves because our regulator is broken. The soul is the regulator that is installed within us, but we have disassembled it and started listening to the ego driven mind instead.

So how do you snap out of a state of *material-comatose*, gain control over your mind, and reconnect with your soul? The first step is awareness and acceptance. Before you even attempt to fix something, you need to acknowledge that there is in fact a problem. Then you need to accept responsibility for it. If you feel that nothing is wrong—if you are in denial—then you are incapable of accepting change and growth.

Are you ready to admit that, at times, your mind may be running wild and out of control? Have you done things, or have you had thoughts that you are not proud of? Are there aspects of your life that you want to change? Before you work on your relationship with others, you must first work on your relationship with yourself.

This is your journey; you only need to admit it to yourself. This is your opportunity to understand your life and to get to know yourself better: do not let this one pass you by too. Don't just read—think and participate. You owe it to yourself to be actively involved in this process. Please physically put this book down and spend some time thinking about this before you continue on.

Welcome back! Now what you need to do is STOP. Just stop! Take a deep breath and stop. You are racing through life and zooming past everything that is important, so stop. Get out of the car, and consciously get out of the race. You need to stop being angry with others, and stop being hard on yourself. You need to stop running from your problems and stop avoiding your issues. Stop the madness, stop the sadness, and stop the chaos.

Tell your mind to stop all its thoughts, and just for a moment, stop creating feelings and emotions. Come to a standstill, and take some time to be silent, so you can understand yourself and understand what you have been dealing with so far in your life. Get to know who you are deep down inside. Trust me, the self-image that your mind has created about who you are is not accurate. Your mind does not have the slightest clue—nor the authority—to tell you who you are. I will come back to this point in the next chapter.

But for now, did I mention that you need to stop? I know stopping everything is easier said than done, but just try. Relax, get comfortable, and become silent on the inside. Don't focus on any thoughts; don't focus on your breath; don't focus on anything—simply practice being silent. Your intent and your will are much more powerful than you think. Get harsh with your words and your mind will follow your instructions. Even if it is just for a few minutes, take a deep breath and let EVERYTHING go. Practice this for a few moments each morning and every night. If your mornings and nights are hectic, then take a few minutes to sit and be silent in your car, or do so in the restroom. Be creative, and I'm sure you will find a way to gift yourself with a few minutes each day.

Before proceeding, please think about what you have just read and answer the following questions?

1. Yes or No. Are you in debt?

2. Yes or No. Do you know exactly how much debt you have down to the dollar?

3. Yes or No. Are you in a state of material-comatose?
    If yes
    a. Since when? How long has it been?
        Since high school started

    b. Yes or No. Do you now see this as a problem?

4. Go back and take a look at the questions you answered at the top of this chapter. Yes or No. Were most of the possessions you listed material possessions? of course it would be matarial, i don't possess people wot.
    If yes
    a. In a couple of words, what do you think this says about who you have become?
        I like materials, but the question was worded in a way where of course it would be material

CHAPTER 4: WHO ARE YOU?

Nearly a decade ago, an employer enrolled me in a weekend long course called *Values*. He was unable to attend, and he thought it would be something that would benefit me. Before I share my experience during this course, I need to give you some background on my life.

MY STORY

My parents left their family and friends in India and came to Canada to give their children a better future. I was born in Canada, but I have always been extremely close to my Indian heritage. I was raised in an extremely loving family, and my parents are my role models. I always understood the sacrifices my parents made for our family, and this has pretty much kept me on the straight and narrow.

My home life was basically as perfect as it could get. My friends used to call us the Indian Brady Bunch. However, growing up, outside the home, I faced racism, and I was severely picked on. "Paki go home" was a phrase I heard nearly every other day as I walked to and from school. This attack really confused me because, as a child, all I could think was, *This is my home, and I am not even from Pakistan.* I often made situations worse for myself because I was the kind of kid who didn't just walk away. I stood up for myself and fought back: non-physically of course. I have had that fight in me my entire life, but still I grew up insecure, and probably up until now, I battled with low self-esteem.

I started working when I was 15 years old, so I could help my parents. At the age of 18 my aunt Rupee convinced me to enter the national Miss India-Canada Pageant, and surprisingly I won 1st runner-up. As fate would have it, a few months later I started to host and produce a weekly South Asian Television show. Shortly afterwards, my partner and I bought five hours per week of FM radio airtime. By the time I was 20 years old my partner had left, and I was running Calgary's largest South Asian entertainment company all on my own.

For years, from Monday to Friday, I worked a paying job from 7am to 11am; I went to University full time, and in the evenings, I managed my radio programs. On the weekends I would write, produce, and host my television program, get sponsorships, create advertisements, do my homework and make time for an active social life. I did not care about money or material possessions, but regardless, I was in a state of material-comatose.

In hindsight, I was doing everything in my power to avoid paying attention to my underlying sadness and sorrow. I spent many of those years battling depression, for no obvious reason at all. I had a great family and a good life, but something on the inside was really broken and missing. I could not understand it, and I could not define it, so I did everything I could to forget it. A state of material-comatose provides great distraction.

Around the time that I was about to take that Values course, I had recently graduated from University, and I had managed to snap out of my depression. Not sure how or why, but I felt pretty good. I did my degree in Communications, and I thought of myself as a good communicator. I was one of the first visible minorities to win Miss Calgary the year before, and I also won 1st runner-up and Miss Photogenic at the Miss Canada (Universe) Pageant. I had recently backpacked all across Europe with a friend, and I was given the honor of representing Canada at the Top Models of the World competition in Germany for three weeks. The icing on the cake was that I was engaged to an incredible man. I felt I had experienced a lot of life. I knew who I was, and I had little difficulty expressing myself to others.

So that gives you a little insight into where I was in my life when I registered for this self-help Values course. The three day course demanded twelve to fourteen hours each day with no outside contact. It was all about self-reflection and knowing your values. I have to admit, the first day I did not have a good attitude. I was actually even a little smug. I was thinking, *I know what my values are, and I know who I am on the inside.* I was questioning why I had come in the first place and was thinking that the experience was a waste of my time.

Let me tell you, I don't think anyone in that class cried as much as I did during that weekend. The course forced me to stop. I had no choice but to stop everything and spend all day thinking about the things that I was working so hard to ignore. It sent me on an emotional roller coaster.

I remember the first thing that caught me off guard: as an exercise we were asked to interview each other, and the instructor had provided a list of questions to the interviewer. My group was going to be answering the questions first. Some people were nervous, but I was cool as a cucumber. I felt I was articulate, and good with interviews. After all, I was most proud of coming in first place in the interview portion of the Miss Calgary and the Miss Canada competitions.

So I sat down across from the girl who was acting as my interviewer, and the first question she asked me was, "What do you do?" I told her how I had just finished University; I was working a 9 to 5 job, and I had expanded my entertainment company. She then asked me, "Why do you do the things that you do?" This question completely threw me off track. I had never thought about why I do the things that I do, and frankly I had no idea.

I think I said something lame like, "These opportunities presented themselves so I took them." She then asked me, "What time of the day are you the happiest?" I felt like I had been shot. I had no idea, and sadly the only thing that kept popping into my mind was *I don't think I am ever genuinely happy.* That ordeal opened up an entire can of worms for me.

We did another exercise where the instructor laid out many different pictures, and he told us to pick one or two. We were to pick anything that jumped out at us. Later he asked us to discuss our choices with the class. People before me picked pictures of Fruit Loops cereal bowls, and flowers. They said things like, "Life is colorful and fun just like these picture. It was all light and positive. Guess what I picked? One was a picture of a bloody war battlefield, and the other picture was of an innocent baby smiling. I had no idea why. I went to the front of the class turned over my pictures and just stood there thinking, *Oh my, I am such a messed up person.*

Fortunately and unfortunately, an entire class of strangers got to witness my many breakdowns and breakthroughs. To make a long story short, one of the major things I learned about myself was that I was trying so hard to be humble that I was not allowing myself to appreciate my successes and my accomplishments. I never felt that I was physically beautiful, and then I became a model and won beauty pageants. The entire thing was so ironic and so bizarre to me. I learned that it was okay to be proud of myself and that patting myself on the back would not make me conceited or self-centered.

There is one more thing that happened that weekend that I wish to share with you. It was an exercise we did near the end of the course. I think I benefited the most from this exercise because I volunteered to go first. The instructor turned down the lights and asked me to stand up and close my eyes. He did not tell us anything about the exercise or what he expected from us in advance.

As I stood there with my eyes closed, he asked me in a gentle voice, "Who are you?" I answered, "My name is Gurdeep." He again asked, "Who are you?" I was confused so I changed my answer and replied, "I am Gurdeep." Once again he simply said, "Who are you?" I opened my eyes and said, "I don't understand what you are asking me."

With a very stern tone in his voice, he told me to close my eyes and to answer his question, "Who are you?" This time I said, "I am a woman." He replied, "Deeper inside; who are you?" I started giving answers like, "I am a human; I am a daughter; I am a sister." Each time the teacher simply kept saying, "Deeper, deeper inside; who are you?" I then started to say things like, "I am compassion; I am strong; I am love." I don't even know what I was saying, but because my eyes were closed, with every answer I felt like I was moving deeper and deeper inside of myself.

I honestly got to a place that felt like the inner most part of me. It was a place where there was not an iota of fear or doubt. I felt peace, clarity, and calmness like I had never experienced before. For a moment, I had forgotten where my physical body was. It was a sensational and almost intoxicating feeling.

Afterwards, I realized that this exercise gave me a glimpse into my soul. I recognized that the soul is where peace, happiness, and true wisdom reside. I was convinced that, when I die, this is the feeling that will surround me. Having always been afraid of dying, this insight gave me such a great sense of comfort and relief.

The course was life-altering, but now that I look back, it only scratched the surface for me. Unfortunately, I was not ready to continue on my spiritual journey at that time. I quickly got back to work and got wrapped up in planning my wedding. I slowly slipped back into my mental state of material-comatose. That feeling went away, but at the back of my mind I always remembered what connecting to my soul felt like.

As amazing as that exercise was—that brief glimpse into my soul—at the end of the day that's all it was, a glimpse. It did not give me awareness of my soul, and it did not provide a long-term solution to my problems. In order to permanently change our lives, we need long-term solutions. We need to be able to connect to our soul every single day, 24 hours a day, on command.

More importantly, we need to create a balanced relationship between our mind and our soul. Again, I think the ideal situation in every human being is to have their soul guide the thoughts and the emotions that their mind creates and the body physically experiences. Only then can we truly live a peaceful, well-balanced, and meaningful life.

I now know that I consistently battled low self-esteem because I allowed my mind to define who I was. The self-image that the mind creates for us is completely inaccurate. The mind does not have the slightest clue as to *who you are*, and it does not have the authority to tell you either. This is why the majority of us do not know who we are. This is why we are constantly trying to become someone or something we are not. We copy and try to be like other people, because we think, *That is the type of person I should be.*

If you do not know *who you are*, you are more likely to try and become like someone else. This is why some people want what other people have. By having what someone else has—whether a material possession, a lifestyle, or a relationship—some people feel like they can increase their own self-esteem. They think that by copying someone else's sense of style, stealing their friends, or by having an affair with their spouse they can acquire a piece of that person's happiness and/or success. To different extents this is why society turns ordinary people into celebrities and role models. Celebrities and role models create stencils for who we should be.

The mind is filled with so many illogical and negative thoughts that it is no wonder people act inappropriately at times and do things that they later regret. It is no wonder people are so hard on themselves. The mind is running free without any guidance from the soul. It is confused, and it has no idea *who you are* or what you want to be, so it keeps creating different images and expectations for you to try and live up to.

The mind is also very naïve and impressionable. Whatever images you see in the media, and whatever expectations society places upon you, are internalized, and your mind accepts them as fact. If you are a woman—doesn't really matter what age—and all you see on television, on billboards, and in magazines are rich skinny women with designer clothes, then your mind starts to develop those images and expectations for you. Your mind tells you, *That is who you should be.*

You work so hard and struggle to become that person, and then you beat yourself up when you cannot live up to these unrealistic expectations. Even if you achieve that goal—and you become like that person—your mind will still not be satisfied; it will create a new set of expectations for you. Your self-image will keep changing… and changing… and changing. You will never truly know *who you are.*

Who you are and what you do is not the same thing. The things that you do, do not define who you are. In order to know *who you are* you have to let go of what you do, and you have to let go of who you think you are. In order to figure out who you are, you have to figure out who you are not.

In the Lankavatara Sutra, there is a Buddhist teaching that states "Don't look for what is real. Just let go of all that is unreal, and that which is real will come to you all by itself." This is a beautiful quote that hits the nail on the head. Who you truly are is hidden behind layers and layers of false ideals and false images. In order to truly know *who you are*, you need to let go of everything that you are not.

I believe that *who you are* does not come from your mind; it comes from your soul. Your soul is old. It is wise, and it knows exactly who you have been, who you are, and what you have the potential to become. No matter how much people or society try to sway your soul, they cannot—the soul is deeply rooted in you, and it is deeply rooted into the creator of you. In order to live an authentic life, you have to figure out who you are, and then become that best you that you can be.

Before reading the next chapter, take a few minutes to reflect on your own life and answer the following questions. Please do not skip this step. Again if you do not know the answer to a question write down, "I don't know." I will help you find the answer as we proceed.

1. In a few sentences describe what you do?

   I am a student studying finance at UofC in the hopes of being a portfolio manager

2. Why do you do the things you do?

   So I can become a portfolio manager and be financially secure

3. What time of the day are you the happiest? *time*

Morning, due to the day of possibilities

4. Yes or No. Are you happy?

5. List a few things that you thought you were, but over time have realized you are not?

Basketball, hood, gangst, dancer, Womanizer

6. Who are you?

I dont know

7. What are you meant to do in life?

To be the happiest I can be

8. What is your purpose?

I dont know

9.   Why are you here? Why do you exist?

I dont Know

CHAPTER 5: FIND YOUR WORTH

Who you are and what you are worth are two things that go hand-in-hand on the path to self-discovery. While *who you are* is a direct correlation to your soul, your worth is determined by how much value you assign to who you are. Your self-worth determines how you perceive yourself and how you think others perceive you. It is how you treat yourself and how you allow others to treat you.

Worth is defined as: *The quality that renders something desirable, useful, or valuable; quality that commands esteem or respect; merit.* Everyone, at some point or another, tries to figure out how, when, and where they are desirable, useful, and valuable. As human beings we look for qualities, characteristics, and traits that command esteem, respect, and merit—from within ourselves and within others.

We have all been taught how to assign worth to monetary things, and sadly we turn around and use that same skill set to assign worth to ourselves. In the monetary world, the more you have, the more worth you hold. As I have already stated in Chapter 4, in this busy, *material-comatose* world, many people associate their financial worth with their self-worth. Often esteem, respect, and merit is commanded through money, power, and success.

When it comes to monetary worth, different people handle money and success differently. If you do not have a strong grasp on *who you are*, the mind goes absolutely crazy when it gets fed worldly success. Money, fame, power, status and material possessions all work like an intoxicating drug that can provide a false sense of ecstasy and joy. While on this high, people act and react in ways that they normally would not. Some people's achievements and accomplishments feed their egos and they completely lose sight of everything else. They become self-centered, egocentric, and vain. They carry a smug persona, and their snobbish attitude makes them talk down to others.

Think about it, how many people do you know whose personalities changed after they came into money, power, or success? How many supervisors and managers do you know that are power trippers? Leaders who take their job superiority to mean that they are better than the people they lead. This happens in every single field. There are many teachers, psychics, charity workers and spiritual leaders that are elitist as well.

Monetary worth does not equal self-worth, and eventually one is forced to face this reality. Deep down inside this truth keeps lurking and lingering until it is dealt with. Often this leads to an inferiority complex within people, which drives them to behave in an even more self-centered and irrational manner. Eventually narcissistic attitudes impact people's relationships and their success. If someone feels that they are not worthy of all that they have achieved and received, they lose control. I believe this is why some people self-destruct. This is the root cause of why people sabotage themselves. Sadly this is what happens to many celebrities and role models.

On the other end of the spectrum, there are other people who legitimately fear success and financial gain. They are so afraid of becoming— or of being perceived as—arrogant, self-centered, and proud that they tell themselves from the very start that they are not worthy of it. Being humble and being self-deprecating are two very different things. Take it from me. This was something I personally battled with for many years.

Growing up, my extended family perceived me as simple and naïve. I was awkwardly tall and awkwardly social. I don't think anyone expected extraordinary things from me. In elementary school—from the first through the sixth grade—I was very torn between my loving and caring home life and my school life, where I was picked on and had no friends. As a result, I had difficulty focusing on my studies. Consequently, I became a poor student.

I made friends and became popular as the years went by; however, my early childhood experiences put me a little behind academically. I had aspirations of becoming a Dental Hygienist in high school. I will never forget my 12th grade homeroom teacher telling me, "Dental Hygiene requires you to pay attention to detail. You should have more realistic goals for your future."

Ever since my siblings and I were children, my parents talked about us getting university degrees. Degree, degree, degree was all we heard. Once, in high school, I nearly failed an exam that I studied hard for. I came home upset and told my parents about what had happened. Later that evening my dad—with love filled intentions, of course—said to me, "If you don't think you can go to university why don't you do a course or something." I was shocked at his comment, and I was heartbroken. I felt like he stopped believing in me.

All of this lit a fire underneath me to become educated, successful, and prosperous. More than anything, I wanted to prove that I was worthy of everyone's love and respect because I didn't think that I was. As I am writing this, I am having a painful realization at this very moment. I am not sure when, but somewhere along the line, I stopped believing in myself. I stopped being worthy of my own respect. I stopped being worthy of my own love.

Shortly after my high school graduation, as I mentioned before, my aunt convinced me to enter the Miss India Canada Pageant. Surprisingly I won 1st runner-up. This opened the door for me to start hosting my own weekly South Asian television show. People's perception of me started to change. I often noticed people recognizing me, and boys looked at me differently; however, this did not change the way I perceived myself.

I constantly told myself things like, *Don't you dare get high on yourself. You are nothing special. You got lucky. You don't deserve people's admiration.* When fans of my TV show approached me, I became uncomfortable and awkward. I was always polite and gracious on the surface, but deep down, I could not accept their compliments. I could not accept their affection. I didn't feel like I was worthy of it.

It became an aspiration of mine to represent Canada at the Miss Universe Pageant, simply because I had always viewed it as an unimaginable dream.

It was something that other women did, not something that I could possibly do. Being a visible minority and someone who battled racism and discrimination, I wanted to prove that anyone could achieve anything if they put their mind to it.

Another reason I joined pageants was because it was my father's dream to see me become famous and successful. My dad used to say, "Now you are known as my children, but one day I want to be known as your father." He wanted me to go to Miss Universe. He wanted me to become a model and an actress, which is very liberal thinking for a traditional East Indian father. I desperately wanted to make him proud.

I did extremely well at pageants and started modeling, yet I felt like I was not pretty enough, not skinny enough, and not good enough. I sincerely felt like I won Miss Calgary and 1st runner-up Miss Canada solely because of my personality and talent. I was flabbergasted when my name was called as Miss Photogenic at the Miss Canada pageant. I remember I just stood there until someone beside me nudged me and said, "Go they just called your name!"

At the time, my mind would not even allow me to think about, or process what it meant to win this title—a title which is based primarily on looks. This win gave me the title of Top Model Canada, and within a month I was sent to Germany to represent Canada at the Top Models of the World competition for three weeks.

When I arrived at the airport in Germany, no one approached me. I was the only relatively tall young woman that got off the flight that looked somewhat like a model. I stood there as the entire plane emptied out. I then saw a couple of people holding a clipboard that said, 'Top Models of the World.' I walked up them and asked, "Are you here to pick me up?" With wide eyes they looked me up and down and with disbelief in their voices they simply said, "Canada?" It was the funniest thing. I remember biting my lip to stop myself from laughing out loud. It was written all over their faces that they were thinking, *but you are brown.*

I think I confused everyone I met on our tour by wearing the Canada sash. Near the end of the trip one of the girls finally spoke up and asked me, "Is everyone in Canada dark skinned?" I smiled because I knew she meant no disrespect. She simply voiced what everyone else was thinking. I eventually explained to all the girls that Canada is a multicultural nation, and how I was one of the first visible minorities to be given this honor.

The daily questions and comments about my ethnicity gave me an outlet. I was able to focus on something besides showcasing my beauty, and I was thankful. I could not even begin to internalize the meaning behind this competition. I could not fathom what this said about who I was and what I was worth.

As my success grew, so did my self-deprecating inner-voice. I would look into the mirror, come face-to-face with myself, and tell myself that I was ugly. I am embarrassed to admit it, but when I went out with all my beautiful friends, I would often go into a washroom stall and cry. I felt so unattractive by comparison. Eventually, I started to avoid mirrors. I didn't like talking about my experiences or my accomplishments. I had trouble accepting compliments, yet I would internalize every negative comment that was said about me. I would say those same mean things to myself non-stop. They echoed and bounced around my head over and over again. It got so bad that I developed an eating disorder for a few months.

I have spent a lot of time thinking about eating disorders and about what causes one to deprive him or herself, in order to look a certain way. I don't think that bulimia and anorexia is about losing weight. It doesn't have anything to do with body image at all. I think it's about punishment. It is self-inflicted punishment, which stems from not knowing your worth and from feeling unworthy.

Think about it; bending over a toilet and jamming your finger into your throat to forcefully throw up undigested food is abuse. Having chunks of food come up and splash you in the face is one of the most humiliating things that could ever happen to you. The sad part is that there is no one else in that washroom but you. You are humiliated, embarrassed, and disgraced all by yourself—in front of yourself. It is gut-wrenchingly sad.

Some people starve themselves, some people overeat, some people cut themselves, and others abuse drugs or alcohol. Regardless of the method, these are all forms of punishment. Without a doubt, self-inflected pain is far worse than any pain an outsider can cause you. When you hurt yourself physically, you turn your back on who you are internally. When you abuse yourself, you further deteriorate your self-worth.

If you have never been in this dark place, it may be difficult for you to understand how this could happen to a person. You may not understand how a person can self-destruct. It is not something that happens over night. Emotional issues typically start off with being hard on oneself, having high expectations for oneself and then getting really upset when you fail. Most of us have experienced, to different degrees, other people saying mean things to us. Things like—You are stupid, or you're no good, or you won't accomplish anything. We internalize other people's perceptions and process them on a deep level. Slowly but surely, most people start to speak to themselves in this manner. This turns into—*I am stupid,* or *I am no good,* or *I am not going to accomplish anything,* or *I am not worthy.* This is how people become self-deprecating and self-loathing.

Now when you are upset with someone, or if you do not like someone, you may lash out at him or her. A point may come when you leave that person and you stay away. When you are upset with yourself and you don't like yourself, what are you supposed to do? How do you lash out at yourself? I think, when emotional beatings are not enough, they turn physical. When punishing yourself with words is no longer enough, and the frustration builds up so much, you then start to punish yourself physically. When you reach this breaking point, the only thing left is to pick your poison. Some people eat, and some people starve themselves. Some people abuse drugs or alcohol, and others cut themselves. The diseases are all different, but I believe the root cause is all the same.

Shockingly, suicides are the primary cause of violent deaths in the world. Reportedly over one million people take their own lives each year across the globe. The suicide rate has increased nearly 60% since 1950. Who knows how many thousands, or even millions, of others attempt suicide each year but fail to die. This has become a pandemic seriously affecting the human race. Humans have evolved from animal species, but have you ever heard about an animal punishing itself or trying to kill itself? This is not a part of the evolutionary process.

I believe that animals are deeply rooted into their souls. Their mind, body, and soul relationship is in harmony. Human's struggle because of our evolved minds. Human intelligence has developed so much that the mind figures it doesn't need the soul anymore. Instead the mind creates an ego and follows its lead. In ego-mode humans are driven to create a life of dysfunction and confusion.

This is what happens when your mind and your soul are disconnected. They become two separate identities who work independently. Your mind and your body go through the motions, and your soul witnesses it. I was punishing myself because I did not feel worthy. I created a self-deprecating voice to punish myself internally, and when that wasn't enough, I chastised myself physically.

People often told me that I was pretty. Pageants publicized my beauty. Photographers and modeling agents reinforced that I had the 'it factor', but none of that mattered. It didn't matter what anyone said because I did not believe those things about myself, and I worked very hard not to allow myself the possibility of believing them. I became a successful businesswoman, and I graduated university with nearly a 3.3/4 overall GPA. However, I never stopped for a moment to pat myself on the back. I never felt proud of myself. I never felt happy.

My monetary-worth and my self-worth were so deeply disconnected that they left a gapping whole inside of me. I didn't think my success was worth anything, and I didn't think that I was worth anything. The first step to my recovery was discovery. It is very difficult to fix something if you do not know what the problem is. I thought that I was a humble person. I never realized that I was being self-deprecating. I did not know that I was punishing myself. I always thought other people hurt me. I did not realize that I was hurting myself far more. Simply recognizing that this was my issue solved half the problem in itself.

As I mentioned in the previous chapter, the Values course I took made me stop and internalize that I was not appreciating my success. I eventually realized that it is not only okay but *necessary* for me to congratulate myself. I needed to be proud of my accomplishments. Doing so did not make me conceited or egotistical. Eventually, as I continued on my spiritual journey and connected with my soul, I recognized how beautiful and special my soul is. I think beauty is not just skin deep; it is soul deep. I realized how beautiful, unique, and special I am because I am a direct extension of God.

Another mistake people often make in regards to determining their self-worth is that they look to their family, friends, and society to define their worth for them. If family and friends are proud of them, then they are proud of themselves. If someone believes in them, then they believe in themselves. If people love them, then they feel loved.

This is an enormous problem because, in this manner, you give away all your power. You give other people the ability to make you feel worthy, but you also give them the power to make you feel unworthy. Someone can put you on a pedestal and make you feel wonderful, and that same person can single-handedly knock you off that pedestal, making you feel worthless, and ruin you emotionally.

This can also open you up to be taken advantage of. Predators primarily target vulnerable people. Vulnerability stems from self-esteem and self-worth issues. By not defining your own worth, you give other people the opportunity to play on your insecurities. Someone may tell you what you want to hear and boost your ego because they are trying to get something from you. They may use you for selfish reasons such as sex, money, drugs, or revenge. They may also manipulate you into going down a path that you would otherwise stay clear of. This is why it is vital for you, and only you, to control the power that determines what you are worth.

On the flip side, if you are a person who often manipulates others, recognize that this also stems from not knowing *who you are* and what your worth. Praying on someone else's weakness is a reflection of your own internal weakness. People who are grounded and deeply rooted into their soul do not manipulate others. The soul simply does not create such intensions and actions.

When you lash out at others and hit below the belt in verbal altercations, believe it or not, you are expressing your own pain and confusion. Happy people do not attack others. Happy people do not insult others. Unhappiness comes from not feeling worthy; therefore, you criticize others, say horrible things that you often do not mean, and find faults in the people around you. All of these actions are a cry for help, which has been distorted by the ego driven mind. Hurting others when you are hurting yourself is dysfunctional behavior, and dysfunction is the ego's specialty.

Before you project an emotion outwards, you must first experience it, and know it on the inside. This is the only way that your feelings and actions will be genuine and consistent. Before you can have compassion for others, you must have compassion for yourself. Before you can trust others, you must trust yourself. You can only have patience for others, if you have patience for yourself. In order to genuinely compliment others and be happy for them, you need to be able to compliment yourself and be happy yourself.

It is so easy for people to say things like, "I love my house," or "I love my car," or "I love that handbag." It is also so common for people to say, "I love you" to other people. However, it is often so difficult to say and accept that you love yourself. The harsh reality is, if you do not love yourself, you cannot expect anyone else to love you. If you cannot love yourself, then you cannot truly love anyone else. It is as simple as that.

So how do you learn to love yourself? You learn to love yourself by learning who you are, and by learning what you are worth. Venturing on a spiritual journey is definitely a step in the right direction, and connecting with your soul is a great place to start—which I will discuss in great detail in the next chapter.

I have found my worth, and I now know that I am worthy of every good thing that comes into my life. Although it is an ever-evolving process, it is my sincerest wish that you will find your worth by the end of this book.

Take a few moments to answer the questions below. I simply want you to start thinking about these things. We will explore them in more detail in the coming chapters.

1.   Yes or No. Do you love yourself?

2.   Yes or No. Do you feel 100% worthy?

3.   Yes or No. Do you appreciate your success?
     If yes
     a. Write down the successes you are most proud of.

4.   Yes or No. Do you associate your material worth with your self-worth?

5.   Yes or No. Are you a person who has allowed your success to feed your ego, which made you act in ways you are not proud of?
     If yes
     a. What have you done that you now regret?
         act like a bigshot
         at cnns

b. How does this make you feel?

— like a foolish kid

6. Write down some of the self-deprecating things you have said to yourself.

— your fucking useless
—fucking waste time
— what have I done today
—why are you always fucking late

7. <u>Yes</u> or No. Are you a person who punishes himself or herself mentally or physically?

8. Yes or No. Are you a person who allows other people to define their worth for them?

If yes

a. Write down who these people are.

Mom, dad, Michelle, erica, mitch, michael, Ana, Maurico, steph

b. Write down a few ways they make you feel worthy.

Include me in social plans
complimants m

c. Write down a few ways they have made you feel unworthy.

Exclude me or forget about me

9.   Write down a few things you have learned in this chapter.

-That I am the
only person to juqge
my myth

-I am in control
of how I see
  myself

-I determine who I am

CHAPTER 6: CONNECT WITH YOUR SOUL

If you are not connected to your soul, then by default you are connected to your mind. If you are connected to your mind, then you are without a doubt allowing your ego to guide you. You are living in ego-mode. When you are living in ego-mode you are completely irrational and dysfunctional. So what do you need to do to completely transform your life? It's simple. Separate the ego from the mind and then connect with your soul.

Connecting with your soul is like reconnecting with an old friend. If you choose to stay in constant contact with that person, you need to build a relationship, and relationships take effort. This is not something that can happen instantaneously, but I promise eventually it will come naturally to you. You won't always have to put so much work into it. Here are some things you can do to take yourself out of a state of material-comatose: silence your mind, connect with your soul, and live a much more fulfilling and meaningful life. The following is exactly what I did, and it worked!

1. TAKE YOURSELF OUT OF AUTOPILOT

Stop going through the motions of life without giving them much thought. So many of us spend the entire day so busy juggling work, our homes, our finances, our family, and our friends that we hit the pillow at night completely exhausted. The few minutes we get to ourselves we spend thinking about all of the things that need to be done, and/or we numb our brains with a few hours of television.

The next day the same routine is repeated, and then the next day, and the next. Eventually we know our routines so well that we just do the things we have to do. We don't really focus on them, and we stop processing them internally. We create a tunnel vision for ourselves, and we stop seeing much of anything else. As I discussed before, this puts us in the mental state of material-comatose.

When you are in a state of material-comatose, it doesn't take long before you check out and put yourself on autopilot. You are simply going through the motions of life, but not truly taking charge and controlling your day-to-day life. Think about a period in your past where you were extremely busy, stressed out, and had too many things on your plate. I bet, when you think back, there are actually very few details that you can remember about that specific time.

After my marriage, I spent two and a half years running a flagship store that carried luxury Jewelry. Career-wise it was the most amazing opportunity. I had a lot of financial gain and success from this job. However, I was so incredibly busy and stressed out during this time that I do not really remember it. I mean, I remember working really hard. I remember my staff, the job, and being spread really thin, but not much else. I don't remember what the summers and winters were like. I don't recall what I did on my days off, or how I celebrated holidays. I have no idea where those two and a half years went.

I think that, when we are under tremendous pressure and stress, we are preconditioned to subconsciously cope with it by separating our inner-self from the situation. In order to protect our soul and our sanity, our inner-world detaches from the outer physical world. Your inner-self—which is primarily your soul—hangs around hoping and praying that you will eventually snap out of your current situation. It patiently waits for you to take yourself out of autopilot and once again take charge of your life.

Often people who have lost a loved one, or people who have suffered a traumatic event, say that the period they spent grieving and healing is a complete blur to them. Again, in order to protect ourselves, something other than our soul and our consciousness takes over. We check out, and our bodies simply go through the motions of life. Physically we can accomplish wonderful things in this state and, on the outside, be incredibly successful; I was the youngest person to ever run a flagship store, and in my first year, I won the company honor of receiving the Management Excellence Award.

However, living in autopilot creates a gigantic oozing wound on the inside. This can go on for years and years unless something is done about it. Luckily something inside of me finally woke up and realized that I did not want to live to work, I wanted to work to live, so I took a leap of faith and quit my job. While I was at home taking some time off, I could physically feel my face unfreezing and my body relaxing. Internally I actually had the time to listen to my thoughts and feel my emotions.

You have to start being actively involved and aware of everything that you do throughout your day. You do not have to quit your job or sit at home to do this; however, you need to consciously make the effort to wake up! Take charge of your life. Otherwise you will wake up one day, maybe in your old age, and think *Where did my life go?*

Take a few moments every morning and every night to check-in with yourself. Think about how you are feeling, assess the choices and decisions you are making, and process the day's events. We are constantly checking-in with our loved ones and asking them about their day, or about how they are feeling. It is due time that you start doing the same thing with yourself.

2. LIVE IN THE MOMENT

One of the most profound early realizations I had in my spiritual journey is that I was never living in the moment. I was constantly thinking about what had just happened, or where I had to go next. I have always considered myself a good friend and a good listener. In fact, I am the kind of person who goes into a restroom and strangers start telling me their entire life's story. I have spent a lot of time listening to people, comforting them, and trying to make them feel better; I used to think moments like these were all about the other person. As a good human being, it was my responsibility and my pleasure to help others however I can, but I thought helping others had nothing to do with me.

I would go places and meet people, and although my body was physically there, my mind would almost instantly leave and start thinking about my endless to-do lists. I had so many friends and people around me all the time, but I constantly felt alone and isolated. This all boiled down to not living in the moment, and not making every single moment of my life about me.

I love the saying, "Yesterday is your past, tomorrow is the future, and today is a gift: this is why we call it the present." Every single situation, experience, and circumstance in your life is about you. Life is about sharing every single moment with yourself and/or with others. If you are not living in the moment, then you are not living at all. Think about that. If you are not living in the moment, then you are not living at all!

When I came to this realization I cried. I cried, and I cried. I thought *Wow, how many years of my life did I spend not living?* I missed out on so many experiences and opportunities to grow and learn. I was thankful that I realized this when I did, but I knew that simply realizing it wasn't going to fix the problem. I had to actively make a conscious effort to change.

Now if I am on the phone with someone, in a meeting, or at the super-market and the clerk asks me how my day is, I snap out of my daze and remind myself to be present in the moment. I am nearsighted, so when I go to a restaurant with someone, I take my glasses off and put them on the table. This way I can only see the person sitting in front of me, and I am not distracted by what is happening around me in the restaurant. If I can, I also put my cell phone away to prevent myself from being sidetracked. I try to give every moment and every single situation my undivided atten-tion and my utmost respect.

My life has so much more meaning now. I have experienced so many incredible moments lately, and I have learned so many things from differ-ent people. I was probably experiencing such things before too, but I just didn't realize it, and I let those moments pass me by. What a shame. I defi-nitely know that I would never have been able to continue on my spiritual journey—and write this book—if I did not start living in the moment.

As a working mother, I constantly felt guilty about not spending enough time with my son. When I was at work, I wanted to be at home with him;

when I was home, I was thinking about my job and how much work I had to do. I'm sure many parents feel this sentiment at some point or another, and it is a difficult burden to carry.

By simply living in the moment everything in my life became about quality and not about quantity. By not focusing on work or my to-do lists, I found it easier and much more enjoyable to spend quality time with my son. Now during our playtime, I am much more relaxed and carefree. I find it gratifying to become a child with him, and play with him at his level. I feel like a kid again. I am not worried about being silly, getting dirty, or acting my age. It is pure and simple fun! We can all learn a lot about having fun, being carefree, and enjoying life from the children in our lives. It is such a blessing to be able to release the child within us, even if it's only for a few minutes.

I know it is much better for my son to have four or five hours of my full and undivided attention, than to have twelve hours of my distracted and stressed-out attention. As a result of my attitude, he is much more confident and happy. Because of our special bonding time, he does not cry when I leave him to get other work done.

As hard as it is at times, when I leave the house, I remind myself that I am a good parent. I know that I will make it up to my son when I get home, and I look forward to it. When I am at work, I try to be present there. As a result I am so much more focused and efficient at my job. This creates a much less tense and stressed-out workday. It is a win-win situation all around, so simple and so easy.

The other benefit of living in the moment is that you inadvertently silence the voice of your ego. In *Practicing the Power of Now*, Eckhart Tolle says "To the ego, the present moment hardly exists. Only the past and the future are considered important. This total reversal of the truth accounts for the fact that in the ego mode the mind is so dysfunctional." He says that when the ego is connecting with the present moment, it is not the actual present that it sees. "It misperceives it completely because it looks at it through the eyes of the past. Or it reduces the present to a means to an end, an end that always lies in the mind-projected future."

By simply being aware of what your ego driven mind is doing, you have the power to control it. If you have the power to control it, then you have the power to change it. Throughout the day, in every experience, make sure you are not thinking about the past or the future. By being in the moment, you can separate the ego from the mind just enough to allow the soul to take control once again.

This really got me thinking about the concept of fear. I think most of us are driven by fear to some extent; however, some people are inundated and overpowered by fear. Fear is an emotion that has the ability to recognize danger. It instinctively tells us to flee a situation or to confront it. Because life is so unpredictable, if feels like there is a lot to be afraid of. People fear everything from death, loss, failure to success. If something horrific happened in the past, those memories haunt people and leave them continuously fearing that the same thing may happen again.

In *Fearless: The 7 Principles of Peace of Mind*, Brenda Shoshanna says, "Fear thrives on lies. It weakens the immune system, destroys our basic sense of confidence and well-being, takes us off track, and makes us pray on those who wish to control or attack us in various ways." She also contents that self-hatred is fueled by fear. An extreme form of fear is paranoia. Shoshanna says that paranoia undermines the core of our relationship and it wipes away "the curiosity, playfulness, joy, and love of life that we are born with."

Fear is a major problem that millions, maybe even billions, of people suffer from. Fear is the most powerful and dominating emotion there is because it creates a very physical reaction. It makes the heart beat incredibly fast, and many people get a shortness of breath. It is an emotion that bullies and over powers all other emotions.

I once heard someone say that there are only two real emotions in life, love and fear. If this is the case then I think love is your soul, and fear is your ego. Fear is not an emotion created by the soul; it is an emotion created by the delusional ego, which lives in the past or the future. The soul and the ego cannot coexist; therefore love and fear cannot coexist. If you come from love then you cannot come from fear. Once again, as Eckhart Tolle says "To the ego, the present moment hardly exists." Thus, in order to eliminate the stronghold of fear, start living in the moment. If you live in the moment, you cannot possibly experience fear.

As I am writing this, I am coming to the realization that since I have started my spiritual journey, I have not experienced fear at all. I may get anxious and nervous from time to time, but I have not experienced the paralyzing emotion of fear in a very long time. I have gone from being a person who was drowning in fear, to never experiencing fear again because of this spiritual journey. I stopped living through fear when I started living in the moment. This is incredible!

When you start living in the moment, your relationships will get stronger, and you will learn more about who you are. You will stop feeling alone and isolated. When you are truly present people can sense that, and you will connect with people on a much deeper and more meaningful level. You will start to enjoy mundane things like washing dishes, taking a shower, or driving. I hardly speed in my car anymore because I really enjoy my time behind the wheel. Nothing in your life will feel like a chore or a waste of time when you are living in the moment.

In my opinion, living in the moment is also the number one weight loss trick. Most people binge and over eat without thinking. This happens when you're living in autopilot. I have heard so many people talk about how they ate an entire bag of chips without even paying attention. It's not until afterwards that they think, *Oh no, why did I just eat that!*

I believe that every single component of life is a balancing act between the mind, body, and the soul. Weight is no different. Whatever is happening on the inside is a reflection of what is happening to your body on the outside. Most of us are emotional eaters. Eating is a coping mechanism for problems and issues. Most people eat because they are filling a void—a void which is created by not being happy, not feeling worthy, and from not dealing with the past. As someone who has spent my entire life struggling with weight and body issues, I know that my issues were more internal than external. When every diet and exercise plan fails to provide a permanent solution, why not try a spiritual approach?

In my opinion, losing weight begins with taking yourself out of autopilot and by starting to live in the moment. When you are living in the moment, you will simply make the right diet and exercise choices. There is no way you will eat an entire bag of chips, or an entire box of chocolates, if you are aware of what you are doing every second of the day. In order to permanently manage your weight, you also need to be happy, worthy, and at peace. Together we will get there.

3. STOP READING AND REACTING

Life is filled with situations and circumstances that require our attention and our response. We have all had moments where we handled a situation well, and we have had other moments where we lost our cool and completely overreacted. We are constantly rushed, and it often feels like time is so limited. From a young age, we are programmed to read and react to situations immediately with little or no time to process them.

More than likely as a situation unfolds in front of your eyes, you quickly read the situation. You then decide how you feel about it, and simultaneously you present your reaction to it. Very little thought actually goes into it. By the time you have had a chance to process your reaction and actually think about the situation in a fair and unbiased manner, it is too late. The damage is done, and you cannot take back what you have said or done.

Let's use a verbal altercation as an example. If you have snapped and yelled at another person, a part of you will feel a little bad about it afterwards. However, your mind does not want to feel bad, so it will rationalize and justify your behavior. Your mind will tell you things like, *Well that person deserved being yelled at,* or, *it's a good thing I taught that person a lesson,* or *everyone would have reacted the same way had they been in my situation.*

If you genuinely care about the other person, then you will eventually apologize and make amends. However, if you continue to read and react to situations without giving them any thought, you will likely behave the same way next time a similar circumstance arises. This is why some people spend their entire lives fighting with each another and then making up. You get caught in a vicious cycle.

This goes much further than simply arguing with other people. If you read and react to situations without thinking them through, then you are much more likely to make rash decisions that could permanently affect your life: your boss or co-worker upsets you, so you quit your job; your boyfriend or girlfriend creates an uncomfortable situation, so you end the relationship; a friend or family member upsets you, so you cut them out of your life forever.

You could end up giving into temptation and then suffering the consequences. You may end up cheating on your diet, or cheating on your significant other. You could end up gossiping about people, betraying someone's trust, and/or unintentionally backstabbing a friend. Physical fights, stabbings, murders, kidnappings often happen when people make rash decisions in the moment without thinking them through first.

You have to stop reading and reacting to situations and circumstances. When something requires a reaction from you, take a few moments to process what has happened. Tell people that you need a few minutes, so you can think about the best possible way to handle the situation. There is a reason parents tell children to walk away from conflicts. We need to be reminded of this childhood lesson. Just make sure you eventually walk back and deal with the situation like an adult; avoiding a conflict, and doing nothing, is almost worse than overreacting. The conflict will remain unresolved, your emotions will remain trapped, and the situation will be entombed inside your psyche.

Now I understand that stopping yourself from simply reading and reacting is often easier said than done. I personally still react without thinking all the time, but now at least I catch myself afterwards and try to better myself. Ironically as I was in the middle of writing this chapter, I got into a fight with my husband and I completely overreacted. I sat back down in front of my computer to resume this topic, and I couldn't stop laughing at myself. We are human and we all get upset and go off the deep end sometimes. Although I am pregnant, and I wanted to blame my reaction on hormones, I knew I was wrong and I had to own up to it.

I am simply asking you to be aware of what you do in your life and to be aware of the way you are reacting to your life. It is easier to blame our problems and our conflicts on others, and obviously it takes two to tango; however, you can only control one of the two parties involved. You can only control yourself and what you put forward in your relationships and in your life. Hopefully this awareness will inspire you to make a change for the better. Do it for yourself, not for anyone else. Remember this change is going to first and foremost benefit you.

4. EMPOWER YOUR SOUL

The soul gives our life its ultimate meaning and purpose. As I said before, your soul is very pure, gentle, kind, and wise. In order to connect to your soul, you almost have to shift your attitude and be on that frequency, so to speak. You have to stop being so negative and stop being so hard on yourself. Again, before you can genuinely love someone else, you must first love yourself. Before you can have compassion for the outside world, you have to have compassion for yourself and your own internal world.

We have conversations with our minds all the time. Now it's time to start talking to your soul. Not just sometimes, but all the time. Be aware that you are having a conversation with yourself deep down inside. We start off letters by addressing them, "Dear so and so…" and we start off prayers by saying, "Dear God…" It may sound a little silly, but if it helps, start off your conversation by literally saying, "Dear soul…"

Sure in the beginning you may not be able to tell the difference between having a thought in your mind and actually speaking with your soul, but you will be able to differentiate it faster than you think. These conversations with your soul will bring you tremendous comfort. It will be a feeling that you will not want to let go of.

Your soul has been dominated by your mind, and severely ignored by you, for who knows how many years. It is due time that you empower your soul to take charge and take over. Again, the ideal situation, which will create permanent peace and harmony within, is to have your soul guide the thoughts, feelings, and emotions that your mind produces and focuses on.

The mind will not want to be controlled. At first you will most likely slip back into old habits. At times you will unintentionally allow your mind to regain control, but then just be aware of it and bring it back. The mind will not give up without a fight, so prepare for the battle, and do not allow your mind to bully your soul. Your intent is very powerful, and you can do whatever you choose. Your mind and your soul will listen to you.

So, be aware of your intent, and participate in your thought process. This will give you something to focus your energy on for a while, something that doesn't have anything to do with the material world. You will empower your soul by silencing your mind and by simply putting forth the effort. When you silence your mind, you can hear your soul. I will say it again—when you silence your mind, you can hear your soul!

5. SHARPEN YOUR INTUITION

Humans have five senses through which we receive information. We can see, hear, smell, taste and physically feel the things that exist in our world. Although science does not fully acknowledge it yet, there has been a lot of research done on a sixth sense that exists with us. It is officially called Extrasensory Perception (ESP).

ESP is more commonly referred to simply as the sixth sense, a gut feeling, and a person's intuition or even as clairvoyance. We all have the ability to simply know certain things. We cannot explain how we know them; we just know. When you first meet someone, you may have a gut feeling—either good or bad—about that person; it might be an uneasy or unsettling feeling. You most likely cannot put your finger on why you feel the way you do, and that is why you often ignore it and dismiss it.

Sometimes people can sense that something is going to happen before it actually does, or while sleeping, they have a dream that actually comes true. People will call this a coincidence, but I do not believe that. There is no such thing as a coincidence in life. Every single thing happens for a reason and for a purpose. These gut feelings, dreams, and premonitions are all communicating with us. They are trying to tell us something. They are providing us with information that allows us to make the best possible decisions.

In *The Art of Intuition,* Sophy Burnham states that the root of the word intuition in Latin is *tueri,* which means to guard or to protect. Burnham contends that we all have sudden insights and hunches that we need only awaken to our inborn abilities in order to develop our inner wisdom. I agree that each one of us has this intuition inside of us, but I think it works like a skill. It is a skill that can be sharpened and fine-tuned, and it can become untrained and incompetent.

Think about it, how many people do you know who are very intuitive? They always just seem to get it right. I don't really want to get into psychics and people who can predict the future right now; however, I will say that these people are able to do so because they have honed their intuition to an incredibly high level. We all have this psychic or intuitive ability within us. As you explore it, and practice using it, you will start to sense and receive stronger and more accurate information.

On the flip side, how many people can you think of who constantly make decisions that they later regret? Why do some people keep picking the wrong type of man or woman to be with? Why do some people constantly get cheated and taken advantage of? Why do some people always choose the worst path in life?

These people are not irresponsible. They are not fools. They genuinely believe that they are making the right decisions: until those decisions come back to bite them, of course. Sadly they think that they have learned their lesson, but they end up making similar choices again. They become so upset, confused, and frustrated by their life. They don't understand how they could have been so wrong when it felt so right at the time.

Sometimes we all have a false sense of intuition. A false sense of intuition comes from thinking you are a good judge of character when you are not. Many people get hurt or fooled when they give someone the benefit of the doubt. Now that is a very interesting saying: benefit of the doubt. You gave someone a chance even though you doubted him or her. Have you stopped to think about where the doubt came from in the first place? Why didn't you take that feeling seriously?

Sir Richard Burton coined the term Extrasensory Perception, and he believed that ESP does not receive information from our physical senses, but that it is information received and sensed with the mind. I would respectfully like to make an amendment to Sir Burton's theory. Just like our consciousness and our awareness, I believe that our intuition is not guided by the mind. True intuition is information sent to us by our soul. Once again, this goes back to why it is so vital for us to be connected to our souls constantly.

As I have already explained, the mind is very ill-advised, naïve, and impressionable. It thinks it can do everything and provide you with everything you need—including guiding your decisions. We are living proof that we don't always make the best choices and decisions in life. This proves that what we think is our intuition is actually just our mind having random thoughts and feelings. We need to learn the difference between our mind talking to us, and our intuition or gut feeling telling us something.

Albert Einstein once said that intuition is "the only truly valuable thing." He says, "The intuitive mind is a sacred gift, while the rational mind is only its faithful servant. Einstein was saddened by the fact that "our society honors the servant and has forgotten the gift."

Everything that I am talking about in this chapter is interrelated and goes hand-in-hand. Communicating with your soul and connecting with your soul will really help make this process easier. Next time you meet someone new, or when you are faced with a decision, take a moment to see if you sense something about that person or the situation. Check with your gut before taking action. If you get an uneasy feeling know that this is a sign from your soul alerting you about something.

If that uneasy feeling is quickly relieved by thoughts of, *don't worry it's fine*, or, *he or she is really cute so proceed*, or, *nothing bad is going to happen*, be aware that this is your mind wanting instant gratification. Your mind is trying to make you feel better on false pretenses. Instruct your mind to stop thinking, and put your focus back onto your intuition. Tell your soul you are listening and ask for its guidance. You will receive it. In the beginning if you have a tough time silencing your mind, ask your soul the question, and then sleep on it. You will have a clearer answer in the morning.

It is through your intuition that your soul speaks to you and guides your day-to-day decisions. It is very much a conversation that is meant to go back and forth. Sharpen your intuition by following your gut and acting upon your soul's requests. Your true intuition will never guide you in the wrong direction.

There will be plenty of times when you get a gut feeling about something, but you cannot control the outcome of the situation. That's okay; it is a part of life. There is a reason we are here on this Earth with seven billion other people. Your intuition is simply putting you on high alert, so just be aware and try to protect yourself and your loved ones the best you can. You cannot use your intuition to make decisions for other people.

Personally, I have been in many situations where I get a gut feeling about something, but no one will listen to me. Because intuition does not provide concrete evidence or proof, it is very difficult to use it as a tool to sway someone else's decisions. It may be painful to watch your loved ones make choices that will ultimately end up hurting or harming them—and sometimes their mistakes may impact you also—but again, this is all part of life.

You can only do so much, and you can only control so much. Just do the best that you can, and work with what you have. Don't put pressure on yourself. Being angry or upset about it—or worse saying, *I told you so*—does not change the outcome. It simply alienates you from the people in your life. It is counter-productive, and it will weaken your intuition in the future.

I would like for you to take a day or two to think about all that you have read so far. Focus on all of the steps mentioned above in this chapter and try to implement them into your life. Regaining your intuition and reconnecting with your soul will help you continue on your personal spiritual journey, and help you understand the rest of this book.

Please answer the following questions:

1.   Yes or No. Do you live in the moment?

2.   Yes or No. Do you live on autopilot sometimes?

3.   List two or three situations in which you read and reacted without processing the situation thoroughly:

4.   How did those quick decisions impact your life and make you feel?

5. In hindsight what should you have done in those situations?

6. Write down a few things you would like to say to your soul?

    —Who am I
    — What am I
    Supposed to do?

7. Yes or No. Have you ever had a false sense of intuition?
    If yes

    a. Write down a few times in your life when you were fooled by
        someone or you made a wrong decision.

        cow, it was a
        bad idea, intuition
                    was right

8. Write down two or three times when your gut feeling or intuition helped you.

    − Rims tock

    − exams

    − Social situations

CHAPTER 7: WHAT IS SPIRITUALITY?

It is now time to peel another layer from the inside of our onion and step outside of ourselves just a little bit. Let's talk about spirituality. We know that there is more to our existence then just our individual human experience. Spirituality, then, is the knowledge and understanding that there is more to reality then that which we can see. It is learning and acknowledging the difference between the physical world and the immaterial world.

When I use the term physical world, I refer to everything in our universe that we can experience through our senses. The earth, the sun, the moon, the planets, along with time and space are all a part of the physical world. Mother Nature, all living beings—plants, animals, and organisms—all of our natural and man-made resources and material things exist in the physical world. We can see them; we can physically experience them, and we have solid evidence that they exist.

The immaterial world, then, is everything that is not directly related to the physical world. It is a reality—and I choose that word very carefully—that is outside the realm of worldly or material things. Our body lives in the physical world, but our inner-self (our mind and our soul) is a part of the immaterial world. Spirituality looks inwards, past the physical body, and studies the immaterial world.

In *The Power of Now*, Eckhart Tolle says, "When your consciousness is directed outward, mind and world arise. When it is directed inward, it realizes its own Source and returns home into the Unmanifested." A simpler word for consciousness is awareness. We are already aware of our external life. What Tolle is saying is that when we take our awareness outwards we see the world. When we turn our awareness inwards we realize the source of our existence. I think the unmanifested source of our existence is our spirit.

The word spirit is often used in many contexts. In *There's A Spiritual Solution to Every Problem*, Wayne W. Dyer defines the *spirit* as "the formless, invisible energy which is the source and sustenance of life on this planet." In his book he quotes Saint Teresa of Alvila who says, "Spirit is the life of God with us."

The spirit and the soul are fundamentally the same thing, but are not exactly the same. This is what I think: when a spirit enters the realm of the physical world it changes slightly and transforms into a soul. To recap what was said in Chapter 2, our souls are very large. Only a tiny part of our soul is attached to our body, and the remainder of the soul lives in the spirit world.

I really want to make this as clear as possible. Because we are mathematical beings who understand numbers, please allow me to explain how I attached percentages to this theory. Again, these percentages only serve as an estimated example. No one can ever predict or prove the accuracy of such numbers.

The way I see it, God created spirits as a subdivision of Him or Herself. Before we are born we exist 100% in spirit form and reside in the spirit world. When we enter the physical world and become human, our spirit energy changes form. It is transformed into what we call a soul. Roughly only about 2% of our soul is attached to our body and lives here on Earth. The remaining 98% of our soul continues to reside in the spirit world.

Again, when a spirit enters a living organism that exists in the physical world—the planet Earth—it is embodied within that living organism as its soul. Thus first we are in spirit form, and then we transform into a soul when we are born. When something dies the soul leaves the body. The soul transforms back into its full spirit form and continues living on in the spirit world. Everything starts off as a spirit, but not everything transforms into a soul.

There are other realms and forms in which spirits exist that are different from the soul. For example, people call God "the Holy Spirit." They do not call God "the Holy Soul." God's helpers and negative entities, which are not a part of our physical world, are also called spirits, but they are different from souls. Since I have defined the soul in great detail in previous chapters, I hope this is starting to make sense.

Our individual soul and our spirit represent who we truly are. It is not defined by our physical human bodies. Therefore, spirituality is getting to know our soul and our spirit. A spiritual path or journey, then, is simply the steps a person takes to gain higher knowledge about their soul/spirit, their immaterial reality, and the essence of their being.

Our body takes physical steps to get from one place to another: we often call this going on a journey. Similarly, in order to build a harmonious inner-life, we go on a non-physical, spiritual journey. It is only through spirituality that one can truly experience a connection with his or her inner-self, a connection with the larger reality.

You may ask why spirituality is necessary. Well to begin with, your physical body would simply be an empty shell if it weren't for your non-physical feelings, emotions, and memories. Your physical body can be in a crowd with thousands of people, yet you may feel completely alone and isolated. You can go into the woods, or go hiking on a breathtaking mountain and feel nothing for the nature that surrounds you.

It is your feelings and inner-life that defines and gives meaning to what your body physically experiences. Whether you accept it or not, spirituality is a major part of your existence. It is far more important than your health, your relationships, and your material possession.

If you do not first connect with yourself, then you cannot possibly truly connect with anything else. You may spend years focusing only on your physical experiences, and distracting yourself from paying attention to your inner reality; however, there will always be something lingering and nagging at you. This uneasy feeling comes from deep down inside of you. It is likely asking you to wake up and acknowledge your inner-life. The voices you hear are the voices of your soul. They are the voices of God.

In *Reason for Hope*, Jane Goodall says, "It is arrogant, presumptuous, to think that I might have heard the Voice of God? Not at all. We all do—that 'still, small voice' that we speak of, telling us what we ought to do. That, I think, is the Voice of God. Of course, it is usually called the voice of conscience, and if we feel more comfortable with that definition, that's fine."

The internal voices often start off as soft and gentle reminders. If you do not listen they get louder and more persistent. I think that a lot of people wait until these soft voices become large, echoing screams before they start to pay any attention to their inner voice. Sometimes harsh, shocking things have to happen to a person physically before they turn inwards. People wait until they are jolted by life before they embark on a spiritual journey. This is what happened to me. You can save yourself a whole lot of heartache and turmoil if you start listening to these voices.

As you become more in tune with your spirituality, you become more connected with the human race, with nature, with the universe, and with God. It's like a game of dominos. All the pieces are already divinely set up into position for you. All you have to do is make the effort to knock down the first domino. Everything else will easily follow behind.

Whether you realized it or not, all the previous chapters were about spirituality. If you have been following along and applying my words to your own life, then you are already venturing on your spiritual journey. Silencing your mind is spirituality; connecting with your soul is spirituality; knowing who you are is spirituality, and so is trying to define your worth. However, as you will soon find out, it goes far beyond this.

Thoughts. Ideas. Questions:

Things are in their,
but I know what they
are, connect them
together now

CHAPTER 8: THE UNIVERSE AND THE SPIRIT WORLD

The word *universe* is simply a scientific term that refers to where the Earth lives. We live on Earth and the earth, the sun, the moon, the galaxy all exist in the universe. However, today the word universe has taken on another whole different meaning. Lately I have noticed that the word universe is being associated with things that have little to do with science, and more to do with spirituality.

You may have heard statements such as, "Ask, and the universe will deliver," or, "put it out into the universe," or, "the universe has been kind to me lately." Some of these associations may have come from astrology, but a lot of books and self-help teachers are taking this human/universe connection to another level. After researching the cosmos and studying the science and the theology of the term universe, I realized that it has countless definitions. It is a word that has taken on a new meaning.

Thanks to literature, the Internet, satellite television, and social media the world is becoming more and more connected. We are truly becoming one global society. Multiculturalism exists in most countries, and we all have the right to our own views and opinions. If someone wants to appeal to masses of people, it is crucial that they are politically correct and do not offend a person or group.

I think that a whole new set of words and theories have come into existence because people are trying to be culturally sensitive, non-offensive, and politically correct. These new words are wonderful, and frankly necessary, because they do not have any preconceived notions or judgments attached to them. Modern day thoughts and ideas do not have any affiliations with the past, and they are not connected to any complicated historical events. When presented with a new word or idea, people are less likely to have a negative reaction or a strong opinion about the subject.

My entire purpose in writing this book is to define and simplify complex things. I may be stretching a bit here, but simply put, I think that the modern word universe is used as a substitute, or as a replacement, for the politically and culturally sensitive word God. It is genius because you can get your point across without attaching it to any particular religion or cultural belief. You also do not alienate people who are atheists and may not believe in a God. The term universe is broad and general, which allows people to interpret it the way they want to.

There are a slew of self-help books that talk about the universe and how the universe impacts our day-to-day lives. Many theories state that humans are like magnets that attract things from the universe: whatever people think about, ask for, or focus on—both good and bad—the universe will bring it to them.

However, the universe is literally a big bundle of gas, matter, and space. If the universe is bringing us loss, stress, and turmoil, as well as love, success, and prosperity then—call me crazy—there has to be someone or something out there that is making it all happen for us. Someone or something is intricately planning and maintaining all that happens in our world.

I do agree that the universe definitely plays a major role in our existence. It is one of the truths that surround us. It is necessary for us to understand its nature and the way it affects mankind. I have spent the last year or two trying to gain knowledge and understanding about this complex reality. From my understanding, the easiest way I can define the universe in spiritual terms is:

1. The universe includes all that has been created, but not the creator.

2. Someone or something, we have been calling it God, divinely created the universe as a home, school, and playground for living organisms.

3. The universe is the totality of everything that exists.

4. Both the physical world and the immaterial world exist in the universe.

5. Everything in the universe lives inside the realm of time and space. When our time and space runs out—when we die—our mind, body, and soul's connection with the universe is broken.

6. The universe only represents all that happens in *this* life. It has nothing to do with the afterlife.

So the next question we need to ask ourselves is, *does something exist outside of the universe?* My answer is, yes absolutely! Again, the universe is a realm that is defined by time and space, and there is a realm outside of time and space. Remember I told you that Dr. Deepak Chopra said that science's next attempts were to research what exists beyond time and space.

I like to define the realm that exists outside of time and space as the spirit world. The spirit world is, by no means, a new concept. Many religions and philosophers have been talking about the spirit world for centuries. It is a very important element to understanding ourselves and our purpose. It holds a crucial key to understanding what the point of life, death, and the universe is.

The spirit world is where the divine creator has a much stronger presence. Everything that occurs there happens under the direct order of God. The spirit world has no physical form. There is no way to define it, or understand it in human terms. There is no land or planet that physically exists. Humans cannot get into a space shuttle and go to explore the spirit world. The word *world* is used metaphorically.

The spirit world is where the afterlife exists. It is the place where everyone who dies goes. It is also the realm in which God's appointed helpers exist. These helpers are assigned very specific tasks—they help guide and maintain all that exists in our universe, and I will discuss this in greater detail in the next chapter.

Remember, in Chapter 2, I talked about how large our souls are, and about how only our body occupies a very small portion of our soul. The remainder of our soul, roughly 98%, exists outside of the realm of time and space; therefore, the majority of our soul forever resides in the spirit world.

98% of our soul lives with God, with God's helpers, and with everyone who has died and left our universe. All souls and spirits exist together in a way that we are unable to fully describe or understand. We are all connected on a level that we cannot even begin to fathom.

98% of our soul knows everything and understands everything that happens both in the physical world and in the spirit world. We have infinite power and infinite wisdom. However, we are so occupied with the 2% of our soul that exists within our body, that we have completely alienated ourselves from the majority of our soul. Thus have we alienated ourselves from the realities of our existence. It is true that as humans, we are not meant to know and understand everything; however, I think we are meant to know and understand a lot more than we currently do.

To summarize, we have the physical world, the universe, which exists within the realm of time and space. Above that we have the spirit world, which is beyond time and space. This begs the question, *are there any other realms that exist?* No, I am not talking about aliens and extraterrestrial life; I am actually not concerned about that debate in this book. However, I do believe that there is one more realm that exists above the spirit world.

It is the realm of the divine creator. This is where God lives, if you will. It is the realm in which God's power resides in its purest form. Nothing besides God exists there. It is far beyond anyone's understanding and far beyond any description. All the words in the world cannot begin to explain God's power, divinity, and glory. We simply have to accept this as a truth that we are incapable of ever defining or understanding.

Take a look at the diagram below:

This is a picture of a pyramid that represents the hierarchy of realms. At the top of the pyramid is the divine realm of God. Directly below that is the spirit world. In the third line of the pyramid, below the spirit world, is where we exist in our universe. I also believe that there is one realm that exists below us in the pyramid, so to speak. But before we look down, let's look up.

CHAPTER 9: TOUCHED BY AN ANGEL

Several years ago I watched an episode of the Tyra Banks show in which she was speaking to a group of psychic kids. The kids were talking about their individual psychic abilities and how these abilities impacted their lives. I never really believed in these types of things, but I remember watching this program and thinking that these children had no reason to lie or make up such things, for they did not have anything to gain financially or career wise. They were just innocent kids.

In fact, they were talking about how their psychic gifts have actually been a burden to them. They tried to keep it a secret for as long as they could. However, when word got out, they were made fun of and tormented by other children and by their communities.

One particular child's special ability really stood out to me. She said she was able to see spirits, who she called spirit guides. She said that every single human being has several spirit guides that stay with us all the time. Her gift is seeing them and communicating with them. Tyra asked if she had any spirit guides around her, and I think the girl said that Tyra had four or five of them.

Right there on the stage the girl focused and asked the spirit guides for their names. I don't remember what names the girl said, but it looked like Tyra was trying to associate those names with her deceased family members or perhaps her ancestors. The names were completely foreign to Tyra, and she made a joke that they didn't sound like black people's names.

I am not sure if Tyra Banks left her show as a believer in psychic abilities, and I personally just took it as food for thought. I didn't make a judgment about it, nor did I come to a conclusion on the subject. Throughout the years I heard this concept of angels, spirit guides, and guardian angels many times. As I proceeded through my spiritual journey, this realm was the hardest for me to understand, but it eventually provided me with my greatest revelation.

Nearly two year ago, I met a woman at a charity event who is a clairvoyant, a medium, and a psychic. Over time I got to know this woman on a personal level, and she became a friend of mine. She typically never allows a third person to sit in on a reading or a channeling session; however, she felt that my energy was very clean and allowed me to sit in on sessions with my family, friends, and acquaintances.

To make a very long story short, I have seen this woman do some jaw dropping spectacular things for many people. I really started to believe in her powers. I came to the realization that just because I do not understand something, doesn't mean that it does not exist or that it's false.

She says that she sees angels and spirits, often as clear as she sees humans. Since she was a child, she has been able to take her awareness out of her body and go spend time with angels in the spirit world. I often asked her to describe the spirit world. She says that it is a place that is filled with immense love and peace. Being there is like being wrapped in raw pure love. She goes there to communicate with her people—her angels. She says that she often hates having to leave that place to come back to earth.

She has had these abilities since she was a child, and has never broken her connection with the spirit world. Perhaps this is why she often gets confused as to why people don't understand what she is talking about. What I really like about her is that she doesn't feel that she has anything to prove to anyone, and she doesn't care if people believe her or not. She has the utmost faith and conviction, and she knows that her beliefs are real.

She is also a very gifted healer, and her method of healing is Reiki. I had never heard of Reiki before, and it really intrigued me. It is a little difficult to explain in a few sentences, but it is basically energy healing. It is a spiritual practice in which practitioners transfer universal energy through their hands in order to heal and bring a person into equilibrium. It goes back centuries. Many people believe that when Jesus Christ and Buddha would reportedly touch people and heal them, they were actually doing

Reiki. It was developed in 1922 by Japanese Buddhist Mikao Usui. It has since been adapted by various teachers of varying traditions. Diane Stein has a great book on the subject called *Essential Reiki: A Complete Guide to an Ancient Healing Art*; however, you can search Reiki on the internet and find loads of information also.

One day I asked her to come to my home and give me a Reiki session. This was nearly a year and a half ago, but I remember it like it was yesterday. I wasn't a full believer, but I wasn't a skeptic either. As I get older, I find that I don't always have to make a judgment about everything, and I have stopped compartmentalizing things as true or false. I just take them at face value and view them as food for thought, so I was impartial and open to see what would happen in my Reiki session.

When she came over, she told me that my upstairs great room—which is the least decorated, messiest, and most boring room in my house—was filled with angels and white light. We decided to do the session in that room. I went to my computer to play some Indian meditation music called *simran* in Punjabi. The woman giggled and said, "There is an angel sitting right beside you, and she is very intrigued as to what you are doing." I stopped and slowly turned to look beside me. Obviously I didn't see anything and I thought, *Okay then.*

I laid-down on a very comfortable massage table, and I tried to relax. I am typically a very fidgety person. Even during massages, I keep twitching and moving. As she started to pour healing energy into my body, I started to feel extremely calm and relaxed. I wasn't moving at all. Then something out of this world happened.

The woman was standing by my head, and she told me that there is an angel sitting by my feet. As soon as those words left her mouth, almost simultaneously, I physically felt something touch my feet. Because of that touch, I was overcome by an unbearable sensation of what I can only describe as love, joy, and peace all wrapped in one. I'm serious; my body could not physically handle the feeling.

Usually when I laugh or cry, I do it pretty silently, but when this sensation came over me, I literally started wailing out loud. Downstairs my husband had a few hockey friends over whom I had never met. Our house is all open-concept, and you can hear everything that goes on. I was aware that they are sitting in the living room on the main floor, but in that moment, I could not control my reaction. I am not sure how it was possible, but they did not hear me at all.

Normally when I get the slightest bit emotional or teary eyed, I instantly get congested and my nose starts to run. This was the first time in my life that tears were simply flowing out of my eyes, and I had no other symptoms. After that cry, I felt as though a thousand pounds of pressure was released from me. She explained to me that this is an incredibly big deal for the angels also. She said that the angels have been surrounding me and touching me for lifetimes, but I have not been able to feel them and experience them until now.

Throughout the remainder of the session, I kept asking the woman to help me understand what she was seeing. She said that the angels are dropping healing energy into my body. She said that it kind of looks like woodsprites, the white figures that look like jellyfish that kept coming down the screen in James Cameron's movie *Avatar*. In the movie they were called *Atokirina* in the language of that world, and they are seeds of the Tree of Souls that lives on Pandora.

I felt almost weightless during my session. I kept telling her, "I feel like I am floating." And she finally replied, "You are." Then I said, "No seriously, I feel like I am not in my body." And she said, "You're not, you are having an out-of-body experience, and you're taking me with you."

Okay now these are far off things that you just read about or hear about. I absolutely did not believe that it was actually possible to have an out-of-body experience. However at that moment, I was not thinking in a rational manner. I kept opening my eyes, and even with my eyes open, I continuously felt like I was floating around the room. This feeling lasted almost an hour!

After she left, the logical skeptic in me started analyzing what had just happened. I started thinking, *I am not even sure if I believe in angels, and today one touched me and I felt it?* How was it that my husband and his friends didn't hear my crying? I tried to understand how it was even remotely possible to realistically have an out-of-body experience. Didn't it take yogis and monks years and years of meditation to experience such things?

I really wanted to discount what had happened during my Reiki session. I tried telling myself that this experience was just a figment of my imagination, and that there had to be a logical explanation for it all. However the strange thing is that, deep down, I could not contest my experience because I knew it was all true. I am not sure how I knew, and this feeling surprised me, but I just knew that it was all very real. It happened, and I experienced it for a reason.

I spent the next several months trying to figure out if angels really exist and if so, why? What is their purpose, and how do they help mankind. By thinking about what others have said in the past, and through meditating and soul searching, this is what I found:

(I will explain these points in much more detail throughout the book; I just want you to start thinking about these concepts. Don't worry if certain things don't make complete sense. It will become clear eventually).

1. There are over seven billion people in this world: plus hundreds of thousands of animals species. Mother Nature, this galaxy, and the entire universe are all maintained by the single power of God. It is a big job, so God created helpers and assistants.

2. God's helpers are called many different things in different languages and religions. I believe in Sikhism, and in Hinduism they are called *farishtey,* while western religions call them angels and spirit guides. (Again this book is written in English, so I am using the English term angels: this word choice has no correlation to any religion or religious belief).

3. Angels live in a realm that exists outside of time and space. This realm is called the spirit world.

4. Although they are not a part of our physical world, they work closely with all that exists in the universe. They are constantly around humans. They touch us and talk to us all the time, but unfortunately most of us cannot experience or hear them.

5. Like God, angels are pure, wise, and powerful.

6. Because they are God's helpers, they act in full accordance to God's will and order.

7. According to God and the angels, nothing is really good or bad. It is us humans who compartmentalize things this way.

8. Each one of us, regardless of the type of person we are, has a set number of spirit guides—usually four or five—whose primary job is to help take care of us individually. These spirit guides know our soul, and they understand our individual purpose in life.

9. The spirit guides use the assistance of the angels to fulfill our wishes. They divinely orchestrate our lives, and they help us get things done. (I go back and forth using the terms spirit guides and angels. As essentially they work as one unit).

10. Depending on the stage of life you are in, and how much assistance you need, additional spirit guides can be divinely added or taken away from your spirit team.

11. Spirit guides and angels hear our thoughts and our intent. They help us make our wishes and dreams come true. It is up to the individual whether he or she is asking for positive or negative

things. It is the individual's responsibility to determine if these things are right or wrong for his or her life.

12. Spirit guides need to be assigned tasks that are clear and concise. If it serves our higher good, they will make it happen for us. However, if we do not know what it is that we want then they cannot effectively help us.

13. Because spirit guides and angels help us serve our individual purpose in life, sometimes angel-interventions occur. They intervene in our lives, on our behalf, to physically pull us out of situations that do not ultimately serve our higher good.

14. Angels vibrate at an incredibly high level: much higher than the level at which humans vibrate.

15. God has given human beings free will. Thus angels and spirit guides cannot interfere with our free will, or interfere with the free will of someone else.

16. Angels and spirit guides have to lower their vibrational frequency in order to communicate with humans. However, they can only lower their vibration a certain amount.

17. There is a vibrational scale that exists. This applies to humans and to spirits. We can only go so far up and so far down without changing energy forms. Spirit guides and angels are unable to go past a certain threshold.

18. If an individual's free will leads him or her to vibrate below this threshold, then angels and spirit guides have no choice but to hover above and watch that person go down the wrong path. They are unable to guide them and protect them.

19. There are some spirits that are even more powerful and divine than angels and spirit guides. They are basically a direct division of God. In English they are called archangels. Archangels are so powerful that they can subdivide into seven billion and help seven billion people at once: people simply need to call upon them.

20. Archangels are also part of the spirit world; however, they vibrate on an even higher frequency than angels and spirit guides. This is what makes them more powerful.

When I first started to understand that I have spirit guides that are around me all the time, looking for assignments and tasks, I joked about it. I didn't mean any disrespect; I was just being funny and light-hearted. If I couldn't find my cell phone I would say to the angels, "Who needs a task? I can't find my cell phone." Even though I was kidding, I often found my phone right away.

You've got to love satellite television, but sometimes the one channel you want to watch goes down and then it doesn't come back for hours. One day I spent the entire day helping out a friend who was going through a tough time, and I missed one of my favorite shows. I'll admit it: one of my guilty pleasures is the Real Housewives of OC. At night the show repeated again, but due to Murphy's Law, that particular channel was not working.

I waited a few minutes and turned the television on and off but that didn't help. I had a very silly thought; I looked up and said, "Angels, can you do something?" Not a word of a lie, I turned the TV off and on and there was my show. The channel was working! Now this could have just been a coincidence; however, I do not believe in coincidences anymore.

Another day during my lunch hour, I wanted to go and deposit my pay-check. However, I work across town, and I did not know the surrounding areas at all. I got into my car and thought, *I really need to find a Scotiabank, but I don't know where the nearest one is.* I dismissed that idea and decided to go shopping during the lunch hour instead. I figured I would deposit my check on my day off.

I don't know if this has ever happened to you while driving, but sometimes you keep making wrong turns without thinking. As you are trying to turn back around, you end up going the wrong way again. This is exactly what happened to me that day during my lunch hour. I was going to the mall, but I exited onto the highway in the wrong direction. I was looking for a ramp to turn around, but missed the exit and took another series of wrong turns. I was getting mad at myself, *What am I doing?*

Then guess what I saw in front of me: a Scotiabank! There are not that many of them in the city, and I had never been to that neighborhood before. I threw my hands in the air and started laughing. I sat there thinking, *You angels are hilarious and so amazing!*

A few days later, I was thinking that the entire season had almost passed and I had not gone to see an NHL hockey game. On my way to work the next day, I heard on the radio that that evening was the team's last home game, and our Calgary Flames had not made the playoffs. I was thinking it would be nice to go, but then I wasn't sure where we would leave our son, and just thought, *Forget it.* I was also thinking about the fact that I had never sat and watched a game in the lower bowl of the arena.

I went to work and forgot all about this conversation I had with myself. That afternoon, my husband called me and said, "Guess what? My buddy just gave me three tickets to the Flames game tonight, and they are incredible seats in the lower bowl." My husband's friend got tickets from his work and couldn't go, so he told us to take our son. In my entire life no one has ever given us free tickets like that to anything. What are the odds of that happening on that particular day?

After several such incidences, I really started to believe that someone out there was listening to me and fulfilling my wishes. I thought back to all the things that happened to me in my life and how I wrote them off as mere coincidences. I felt so special and so protected. It is amazing to have such an incredible hookup. However, now that I was aware of this, I had to be very careful about what I was thinking and what I wished for.

Before proceeding please answer the following questions. Yes I will say it again, please don't skip past this section.

1. List two or three major coincidences that you have experienced in your life:

2. Yes or No. Do you think that it is possible that they weren't coincidences after all?

3. Yes or No. Have you ever felt the presence of angels or spirits? If yes.
    a. When are where?

b. How did they make you feel?

CHAPTER 10: FREE WILL

There is no doubt that everything that exists is created and maintained by the divine power of God. Every single thing happens in accordance to God, and under his or her command. In the Indian language of Punjabi there is a saying that translates as "not even a leaf can move in the wind without God's will." God is the supreme power, but God has given human beings a lot of power and responsibility also. It is very important to understand that aside from giving us a mind, body, and soul, it is God's ultimate choice to give us free will. It is God's will to give humans free will.

This is yet another fascinating twist in the creation of mankind. Free will is basically the notion that, as humans, we have a choice. We can choose to do whatever we want in life—from selecting the types of food we want to eat, to picking the people we have relationships with—it is our choice. Our thoughts, wants, and actions are all driven by our individual free will.

God does not interfere with our free will, and believe it or not, God does not judge us for our choices either. What would be the point of giving humans free will if every decision and action is being scrutinized and judged? This would make no sense and would serve no purpose. We are a direct extension of God; we carry a portion of the divine light within us, and God loves us. God is not testing us, and is not waiting for us to fail. This is a profound point, and I really want you to think about this.

Neale Donald Walsch, like many of us, always asked God questions. He contends that one day God started to answer his questions. In his book *Conversations with God: an uncommon dialogue*, Walsch says that God said to him, "You are your own rule-maker. You set the Guidelines. And you decide how well you have done; how well you are doing...No one else will judge you ever, for why, and how, could God judge God's own creation and call it bad?" God continues by saying, "A thing is only *right* or wrong because you say it is. A thing is not right or wrong intrinsically."

The purpose of life is not living out a test that we either pass or fail. Life is not an exam in which we either do good or bad. Again, it is us humans who compartmentalize and view things as good or bad; I love the saying, "nothing is good or bad, but thinking makes it so." In the spirit world there is no such distinction; there is no such thing as simply good or bad.

It has historically been proven that humans are incapable of coming to a unanimous decision about what is right and what is wrong. Various cultures and religions differ significantly when it comes to defining what is considered right and what is considered wrong: different countries even have different laws and regulations.

Drinking alcohol is illegal in some parts of the world, and in other parts of the world the government owns and operates liquor stores. Same sex acts are strictly punished in some countries, and same sex marriages are legally accepted in other countries.

Children have to work to make a living in some countries, and in other countries child labor is a heinous crime; however, these countries then turn around and import products made by children from other parts of the world. It is against the law to take another person's life in every religion and in every single country, but the law protects the army when it kills thousands of people during wars. What is right, and what is wrong?

In Abrahamic context the word *sin* is defined as an act that violates God's will. If God gave human's free will then how can we violate His or Her will? In *There's a Spiritual Solution to Every Problem*, Wayne W. Dyer says, "Sin is nonexistent. There are only obstacles to one's ultimate union with God."

Let's leave religion and the law out of it altogether and look at this from an unbiased moral standpoint. If your free will leads you to do things that are harmful or intentionally destructive for other forces in the universe—these include other humans, animals, and the environment—then those choices certainly have consequences. These consequences may come to light in this lifetime, or they may follow you into the afterlife.

Humans have created a ridiculous list of sins for themselves. This list of sins simply creates an environment of control and judgment. Most of them are fabricated and do not make much sense. For example, after a lot of soul searching, I strongly believe that it is not a sin to be homosexual. It is your free will to choose whom you love, and whom you want to be intimate with. If God did not intend for some men and women to have same sex thoughts and feeling, then he or she would simply not have made such feelings possible.

We all agree that everything happens in accordance to God. If God wanted to, then God would have removed homosexuality from our world. Again God is not testing us to see if we will make the right decisions. This is simply not true.

There is a spiritual explanation for this belief as well. The reason why I am so certain that homosexuality is not a sin is because our soul does not have a gender assigned to it. It is not identified as a man or a woman, and there are no male and female sexes in the spirit world. Each individual spirit is based on its own merit and determined by how much love and energy it carries. There are masculine and feminine traits, but these can be present in both sexes: they are not defined by gender.

Yes procreation is an important part of life; however there are a lot of heterosexual couples that choose not to have children and/or are physically incapable of having children. If you believe that homosexuals are committing a sin because they are unable to procreate, then by the same logic, everyone who does not have biological children is a sinner too. Obviously, this is baseless and not true.

You may then ask, *why did God create a man and a woman*? I will address this question in a later chapter. There are several other things I need to clarify first.

My point is that we do not have the right to place judgments upon anyone else's free will. Again, God does not judge, so we need to stop judging also. Like Albert Einstein said, "Whoever undertakes to set himself up as a judge of Truth and Knowledge is shipwrecked by the laughter of the gods." We need to stop judging ourselves, and stop judging the people around us. Prejudices, racism, discrimination, anger and hatred are all paralyzing factors in our world. They paralyze our ability to grow, to learn, to heal, and to unite us as a global society.

The thing that we need to understand and acknowledge is that each one of us has our own free will that we exercise on a day-to-day basis. The life that you are currently living is a direct result of the choices and decisions you have made. Although there are other elements in play, which we will talk about soon, for the most part the situations and circumstances you face are a consequence of your free will. If you want to change the condition or the quality of your life, then you need to change the way your exercise your individual free will.

Please take a few minutes and answer the questions bellow.

Yes or No. Do you judge others?

1. Yes or No. Do you criticize others for their choices?

2. Yes or No. Do you criticize yourself?
   If yes
   a. What do you criticize yourself for?

   b. Why do you think you are so hard on yourself?

3.   Yes or No. Have you ever caught yourself being a hypocrite?

4.   Yes or No. Have you ever felt like a sinner?

5.   Yes or No. After reading this chapter do you still think you have sinned?

6.   Yes or No. Have you ever feared God's judgment?

7.   Yes or No. After reading this chapter do you agree that God does not judge?

8.   Yes or No. Going forward will you stop judging and criticizing yourself?

9.   Yes or No. Going forward will you stop judging and criticizing others?

10. What aspects of your life is a result of your free will?

11. What misfortunes in your life do you blame others for?

12. Yes or No. Do you stand in the way of your own happiness?

13. Yes or No. Do you sabotage things by yourself, just so you are not disappointed by others?

14. Yes or No. Do you use your free will to better your life?

15. Yes or No. Do you use your free will to better the lives of your loved ones?

16. Yes or No. Do you use your free will to help strangers and to better the world?

CHAPTER 11: BLAME IT ON GOD?

Since the beginning of civilization there has been much discussion, debate, and literature written about the divine creator. There has been just as much curiosity and speculation about mankind's relationship with the higher power. It is a complicated and emotional subject, and most people are very passionate about their opinions.

I often think that it must be difficult to be the creator—the God figure—for humans. When things are going well in our lives we often say, "I did this," or, "I accomplished that," or, "My hard work and determination brought me to this point." However, when things happen in our lives that we perceive as bad we say things like, "Why did God do this?" or, "How could God let this happen?" or, "God should have done something to prevent this." When good things happen we take the credit, and when bad things happen we blame it on God. Mostly we only whole-heartedly pray when things are going poorly in our lives. How frequently do we pray and give thanks to God when things are going well? To different degrees many of us are guilty of this: myself included.

Sometimes I think that if natural disasters, conflicts, deaths and all the other horrible things that exist in our world disappeared, then slowly but surely, so would our faith in God. If everything were perfect, humans would no longer need God.

I have personally doubted the existence of a God at times. Perhaps because people with strong faith explain the horrendous suffering in our world as God's will. Wars, terrorist attacks, murders, inequality, and poverty all get blamed on God's will. Children are abused, refugee camps are overflowing around the world, and mass murders occur in conflicts. All this is God's will?

I used to think that if a God truly exists, then how could he or she allow such things to happen? Why does God not fix world hunger, and stop the violence and destruction? Why does God take innocent children and young adults before they have had a chance to live a full life? Why does God only answer some people's prayers and not everyone's? I'm sure many people have had similar thoughts. This is perhaps the major reason why people stop believing in a higher power and become non-believers and atheists.

It is the notion of free will that helped me understand God's will. Again it is within God's will to give humans free will, and it is God's will not to interfere or override anyone's free will. Currently and historically everything in our world has happened not because of God's will, but rather because of human free will. The human race cannot make God the scapegoat.

As a global society, we have to take responsibility for our actions and for the actions that mankind has been taking. The world is passed down, as is, from generation to generation. Unfortunately, each generation has to bear the burden of the choices made by previous generations. However, each generation also has the opportunity to learn from the mistakes made in the past. They have the opportunity to change their free will to create a better world. Sadly though history keeps repeating itself, and today mankind is in more turmoil than ever before.

It is not God who created world hunger. God created enough resources and food for everyone to share. It is the greed and selfishness of mankind that has globally created a situation where some people are forced to throw away left over food into the trash, while others are made so desperate that they pick out food from the trash and eat it. Sure some nations are richer than others, but poverty and inequality exist in every part of the world. Millions of men, women, and children go hungry every single day in North America too. Also millions of people have a lot more than they need in most developing nations.

It is not God's fault that thousands of people die in wars. It is man who created arms and weapons. Humans have always fought battles physically, and we continue to do so. Innocent animals are killed and forced into existence, and our environment is in ruins all because of human free will. We blame God and Mother Nature for natural disasters, but don't you think mankind has had a hand in upsetting Mother Nature's balance? Don't you think that humans have done things to cause natural disasters?

Benjamin Disraeli, who was a British Prime Minster in the late 1800's, famously said, "Man is not the creature of circumstances; circumstances are the creatures of men." From global warming, to animal extinction, to the depletion of the world's natural resources, mankind's fingerprints are all over environmental problems.

I think God hopes that the consequences of our actions will eventually teach us a lesson, that these consequences will awaken us, help us learn, and force us to make a change. On the positive side, I strongly believe that we are in a very exciting time right now because more and more people are becoming aware of this. We are in the beginning stages of a movement that is going to revolutionize our world and the human experience. This is the time to be hopeful and optimistic. As people wake up, reconnect with their souls, and understand who they are and what they have the potential to become, they will change the way they exercise their individual free will.

One single person cannot realistically change the world on their own, but when thousands of people start to make changes for the better, this will certainly have a rippling effect on our world. When masses of people start using their free will in a positive way, it will impact our global society.

Already millions of people are thinking about the environment and their carbon footprints. They have started reducing, reusing, and recycling natural resources and material things. They are getting involved, voicing their opinions, and peacefully protesting against wars, weapons, drugs, inequality, and injustice. People are communicating, sharing, showing compassion, reaching out, and helping one another. They are *paying it forward* by donating, volunteering, and by doing charity work for complete strangers who live across the globe.

So wake up, take a stand, and join the movement! Get involved, and help heal our world. Take the time to consider all your options before you exercise your free will. Before taking action, think through how that choice will impact your life, your society, and the world. Like Mahatma Gandhi said, "Be the change you wish to see in the world."

The concept of free will is a major component in understanding our purpose in life and in answering the profound question: what's the point of life, death, and the universe? However, we are just beginning to scratch the surface when it comes to understanding our existence. Aside from free will, I am also a firm believer in destiny and kismet. Destiny and kismet are basically notions that some things are just meant to be in our lives. They imply that some things are predestined and beyond our direct control. I have spent a lot of time soul searching about how these concepts relate to our free will and our lives. Some of you may be wondering the same thing. I believe I have found answers; however, now is not quite the right time to talk about this.

You may be filled with questions about things that I have not discussed or may have left out. I am aware of this, and I am doing so intentionally. Like a jigsaw puzzle, I have to make sure I bring forth pieces delicately, in a particular order. This is to maximize your potential for spiritual growth, inspiration, and awareness. Rest assured, I will discuss concepts such as kismet, destiny, and the other factors which impact our human existence. By the end of this book, I will bring everything together and hopefully answer most of your questions and inspire you to ask many others. I ask you to stay with me and trust in the process.

It's that time again. Please reflect on your life and fill out the following two questions:

1. Yes or No. Have you ever been upset with God?

2. What have you blamed God for?

CHAPTER 12: GUILTY GRATITUDE

Although I went through phases in my life where I could not understand God and His or Her role in our world, there have been many more times when my faith was very strong. Regardless of the problems I have faced, I have always been tremendously grateful for everything that I have. I was born in North America, I live in a relatively safe environment, and there has always been food on my table and clothes on my back.

When I went to the Sikh temple or when I prayed at home, I felt very guilty asking God for anything, even as a child. I felt like there were so many other people in this world that are in far worse situations than I was in, and those people needed God's attention and His or Her help more than I did. I would pray for other people, but I would never ask anything for myself.

It is human nature to want things, so obviously those thoughts frequently arose in my mind too. I often wanted to complain about certain things that were happening to me, and I wanted to ask for things, but I believed that I should not as I didn't have the right to. Eventually this created an internal conflict within me. I wanted to ask God to give me more things for myself, but I felt too guilty to do so. By wanting to ask for more, I thought I was being ungrateful for all that I already had. It got to a point where I was not only feeling guilty about wanting more, I also started to feel guilty about everything that I already had.

My gratitude was laced with constant feelings of guilt. I often questioned, *Why me? Why do I get to eat, be safe, and have a loving family and not every-one else? Why am I healthy, while thousands of other children and adults are suffering from diseases and illnesses? Why do I get to go to school and take vacations, while millions of people around the world are homeless and living in refugee camps?* Some people have a guilty conscience, whereas I had guilty gratitude.

Growing up, these mixed feelings were heightened by the frequent trips my family and I took to India to visit our family. In North America we know that poverty exists, but it is, for the most part, hidden behind closed doors. In a developing country it is all out in the open for everyone to witness.

I love India. It is a religiously diverse country with strong roots, beautiful cultures, and good values; however, you don't always experience this while walking around in the streets. There are poor impoverished men, women, children and elderly begging for food and money everywhere—and I mean *everywhere*. I saw countless disabled people with all sorts of physical ailments. Frail, weak women would roam the streets carrying children who were clearly suffering from malnutrition.

I even saw tons of people, of all ages, who had no eyeballs in their eye sockets: now seeing someone who is blind is one thing, but to see people with no eyeballs in their sockets was absolutely traumatizing. I then heard that eyeballs are usually removed to help the beggars make more money. Also gangs kidnap children, physically disable them, and make them beg for money as a business. How can one even begin to fathom such cruelty and injustice? I felt very grateful for the life that I had, but more than anything, I felt sad and guilty.

When I was 16, my family and I went back to India and took a cross-country trip to visit Sri Hazur Sahib, which can be equated to a religious pilgrimage site. It took us four days to get there by train. There were nearly 20 of us on this trip, so instead of sitting in the first class—where most foreigners sit—we sat in regular cabins, which are open to everyone. The train was small, congested and it looked like it was a hundred years old. It was painted light blue on the inside, and each cabin had four benches in total—two on top of each other.

India's landscapes and villages were spectacular to see from the train; however, they smelt a lot like manure. It was a smell that seemed to emanate from the land itself, and not from the train's washrooms. I remember, on the first day of our trip, my younger sister went to use the restroom before me, and she came out screaming. My parents were laughing hysterically at her reaction, while I thought someone had attacked her in there. When I went into the stall to check it out for myself, I completely understood her horror. In the washroom, which I cannot call a restroom; there was no toilet of any sort. No exaggeration, instead of a toilet there was a round open hole in the middle of stall, through which I could see the passing train tracks below! Everything everyone did was simply laid out on the open tracks. It was all out there for everyone to see and for everyone to smell. It was disgusting, but it was actually very funny and very memorable. At least we didn't have to worry about the flush getting stuck, or the toilet overflowing.

My family is from Punjab, which is in the north, and it is the agricultural hub of India. Going into southern India, I sadly witnessed even more poverty and injustice. On this trip, I saw a very different side of human nature, one that I had not been exposed to before. Seeing hunger and inequality made me feel tremendously sad, thankful, and guilty, but I found that not everyone reacted the same way. I observed many situations where people were beyond insensitive and downright cruel to the underprivileged.

I can understand that locals and tourists alike get very annoyed and bothered by the beggars. They are relentless and often rude themselves. Also people say that begging is a business in India, which should not be encouraged. However, there are millions of people who live below poverty lines that work hard to earn a living. Shockingly, from what I witnessed, most people did not have compassion for them either.

One day, during our journey, this young child jumped onto our train just as it was leaving a station. I can still see him; he was wearing a white collared shirt that was two sizes too small for him, and it was completely worn out and stained. On the bottom he wore brown khaki shorts and torn up thong slippers. He was a shoe polisher and was walking around the train asking if anyone wanted to get their shoes cleaned. I thought it was ironic that he was a shoe polisher, yet he did not have decent shoes on his own feet.

An elder man in our cabin called the boy over to clean his shoes, and we all started talking to him. He told us that he is seven years old, and has five younger brothers and sisters. He said both of his parents had died, so he works as a shoe polisher seven days a week to provide for his siblings. At seven years old, he works on trains all alone to make money for his younger brothers and sisters. In North America we barely let a seven-year-old walk down the street alone.

I asked him if he went to school, and he smiled and said no. He said he was trying to make enough money so his younger siblings can go to public school. The boy seemed so innocent, so pure, and so honest. He was in an unimaginably difficult situation, yet he had a smile on his face. On one hand seeing this broke my heart, and on the other hand I was so inspired by him.

The entire time he was shining this man's shoes we were conversing with him. When it came time to pay this child for his work this elderly man, who lives in Canada by the way, started bargaining with him. I could not believe it. Instead of giving this boy a huge tip for his hard work, this man was refusing to pay him his worth. Let me tell you the boy was not asking for a lot of money; it was less than a Canadian dollar. When the child dared to ask for more money, he simply got yelled at and was told to leave.

Unfortunately my parents were on the other side of the cabin sleeping, and I had no money on me. Also no one had the guts to say anything to the older man. Looking back I don't think that the older man is a bad person, but his mentality was very different. He was proud of his negotiation skills, and I guess he didn't pay any attention to the boy's poverty. He was able to separate the boy's work from the boy's personal situation.

I will never forget the look of disappointment on the child's face. I watched him go through the train, and everyone spoke to him with such contempt and rudeness for no reason at all. Forget bargaining with him, they simply gave him whatever they wanted and told him to get lost.

It was as if his mere presence and existence bothered people somehow. In hindsight maybe the boy represented everything that is wrong with this world: death, poverty, inequality, injustice, loss of innocence, & child abuse. Perhaps people do not want to be reminded that this is a reality that exists in their world. They would rather ignore and dismiss those thoughts, rather than think about them and acknowledge them. People would rather dismiss him, than think about what he represents. I often wonder where that boy is now and send him my prayers. I wish I had done something to help him when I had the chance. I know I was only 16 years old, but still I wish I had stood up for him. I'm sorry I didn't.

The next day, in the exact same train cabin, I witnessed something even worse. As long as I live, I will never forget this. Every so often the train stopped at stations to pick up and drop off people. While the train is stopped many locals come and try to sell passengers food, toys, and other merchandise. Some of them come directly onto the cabins, but mostly they walk around outside of the train on the platform. They exchange money for the products through the large windows that are barricaded with horizontal steel bars.

One evening, while we were stopped at a station, a little girl walked onto the cabin to sell peanuts. Her jet-black hair had blonde highlights—over-exposure from the sun does that. It was tightly braided into two pigtails that looked like they were done several days before. She was wearing an old dirty green dress that was far too large for her. She was really cute and endearing so we all bought some peanuts from her.

Across the aisle from us sat a heavyset woman who was also wearing green. Unlike the little girls warn out green dress, the woman was wearing an expensive green silk sari. As the girl finished helping us, the woman snapped at her and rudely asked her to bring her some as well. Completely unaffected by the woman's demeanor, the girl got excited about making another sale. She quickly ran off the train to go get more.

This time the little girl didn't get back onto the cabin. Instead she stood on the platform and knocked on the woman's window. The knock caught my attention. Just as the peanuts exchanged hands, the train started to move. The woman took the peanuts, and then decided not to pay for her purchase. I will never forget seeing this woman, who was obviously well fed and well dressed, just sitting there staring straight ahead eating her peanuts, while this poor little girl was running alongside the train begging for payment. The little girl was respectfully pleading with her in Hindi saying, "Ma'am please pay me, I will get in trouble for not collecting payment; ma'am please pay me." The little girl had a lot of will power and she was persistent. This eight or nine year old girl ran along the side of the train for what felt like a very long time, but eventually she got tired and the train picked up too much speed.

The woman was completely unaffected by her actions, and she showed no emotion. I just sat there and watched in utter shock. Again, I don't know why I didn't say anything to that woman. I guess I was so shocked that I couldn't physically react. Till this day, I regret not giving that woman a piece of my mind. I don't know if my words would have made a difference to her or not, but still I should have tried.

Sitting in trains and stations, watching all of the starvation around me, I could barely swallow my food. I did what I could by giving my own food to those in need around me. My parents constantly got mad at me for doing so. They kept telling me that I was being naïve and that we cannot help everyone. My parents are very generous people, but of course they were worried about my health and well being first. I just felt too guilty to eat. I kept sneaking off and giving my food to children.

When we arrived at our destination, I got extremely ill. I had a water infection where my body rejected its own water. I ended up in the hospital and nearly died. Till this day my dad is convinced that I got sick because I was giving my own food away, and I was not taking care of myself. I think someone just accidentally switched my bottled water with tap water, but who knows. Maybe my overwhelmed feelings of guilt had something to do with my body shutting down.

After witnessing such things, I could not possibly come back to Canada and then say, "God I need this," or, "God please send me that." Also I never wanted to become one of those ungrateful people who felt no guilt or remorse wronging and mistreating the less fortunate. I thought I would much rather feel guilty and sad than entitled and unsympathetic like some.

Several years later, I was talking to a very spiritual woman about this exact subject. I had mentioned to her how I feel guilty asking God for anything because I had already been given so much. She was surprised by my statement and asked, "Why?" She told me that she asks God for things all the time. God is like a parent to us, and we ask our parents for things constantly. She said. "If you die not fully satisfied with your life, God's going to say to you, 'you only had 100 years or so, why didn't you ask me for anything?'"

This got me thinking about the notion of praying and asking. What role does it play in our lives, and how important is it to ask for help? It also got me thinking about the concept of guilt versus gratitude. Looking back, I don't understand why I put so much pressure on myself. Gratitude is extremely important in life, but my gratitude always went hand in hand with guilt. Through my spiritual journey, I learned that gratitude should never be mixed with guilt or remorse. It should also never be mixed with entitlement and feelings of superiority. These are all completely different things that really have nothing to do with one another.

Again it is human nature to want things and to want to achieve things in our lives. Whether we realize it or not, we need help to accomplish our goals. I used to think that God is so busy that I should not bother Him or Her with my petty requests. I now know that I am a direct extension of God and my experience matters just as much as anyone else's. Having more or less than anyone else is irrelevant; my life and my journey matters just the same.

I now understand that God has created helpers, angels, and spirit guides, who have been assigned to us individually. Each one of us, regardless of the type of person we are, has four or five spirit guides that stay with us at all times. God has ensured that each one of us is individually guided, protected, and taken care of. If God created seven billion people on earth, think about how many angels and spirit guides He or She must have created to help us. Wow, this is how much God loves us; this is how much humans mean to God!

This was a profound realization for me: a realization that continues to fill my heart with so much pure gratitude, joy, hope, and love. Each one of us is so blessed and so loved! So why is gratitude so important? It is important because it is an expression of love. Actually I think gratitude is simply another word for love. When you feel pure and wholehearted gratitude, you are automatically immersed with feelings of love. It is this love that frees us, opens us up, and allows us to receive more.

Worship is an act of religious devotion usually directed towards a deity. Most religions teach people how to worship the supreme power. My spiritual journey taught me that God does not want to be worshiped or praised. He or She simply wants love in exchange for love. When we are grateful for the gifts God has given us, we are accepting God's love and simultaneously expressing love back. I believe that gratitude is basically the pure exchange of love between humans and the divine creator. Loving God begins with being thankful for everything he or she has given us.

It doesn't matter if your skin color is black, white, or any shade in between. It doesn't matter if you're a man or a woman. It doesn't matter if you're a child, an adult, or a senior citizen. It doesn't matter if you're rich, poor, illiterate, or have earned a PhD. It doesn't matter if you're a simple domestic caretaker or a powerful businessperson. It doesn't matter if you're straight, gay, religious, or non-religious. It doesn't matter if you're a priest or an inmate. It doesn't matter if you live in the slums of India or in the suburbs of the United States of America. Every single one of us is worthy of the life that we have and worthy of all the happiness this world has to offer.

Every single one of us is directly validated by God and is unconditionally loved by God. We are a part of God, so of course God loves us uncondi-tionally. Every single one of us carries a portion of God's light within us. According to God, the spirit world, and the universe we are all equal; we are all incredibly special. No one should feel superior to anyone else; no one should feel inferior to anyone else; no one should feel unworthy; no one should feel unloved because no one is.

Before proceeding please answer these questions. You have been making so much progress; stay with me and all the pieces will come together soon. I can't do it alone; you have to fill in these questions to do your part.

1. Yes or No. Do you feel guilty about your blessings and possessions?

2. Yes or No. Have you ever felt guilty about asking for things?

3. List three things that you would like to pray for?

4. List everything that you are grateful for. Start with your breath, then your heartbeat, and then work your way out. If you need more space there are blank pages in the back of the book.

5. Yes or No. Do you feel unworthy of some things in your life?
   If yes
   a. List what those things are:

6. Yes or No. Do you now understand that your life's experience matters just as much as anyone else's?

CHAPTER 13: LAW OF INTENTION

A lot of self-help books and spiritual teachers talk about the power of thoughts. They say things such as, *thoughts are things*. There is an evolving philosophical theory that says humans are like magnets in the universe, and our thoughts attract things to our lives: both good and bad. If we think negative thoughts, then the universe will send us negative things. If we think positive thoughts, then we will attract positive things. It is the Law of Attraction used in spiritual terms; like attracts like.

Perhaps the best-known book and accompanying film on this topic is *The Secret* by Rhonda Byrne. According to the authors in this book, our thoughts are manifested literally and directly into our lives. This theory also states that it is our thoughts that create the lives we are living. People with great success and money have it because they asked for it, and because they focus their thoughts on positive things. People who suffer, and have difficult lives, are in that situation because they have negative and pessimistic thoughts: bad relationships, money loss, and diseases for example are all attracted by an individual's negative thoughts. Thoughts hold all the power in this theory.

Although *The Secret* has sold millions of copies worldwide it has also been met with harsh criticism. Many people, including Harper Collins author and veteran psychotherapist, Thom Rutledge, have been outraged by this book's theory and over simplification. Rutledge says that the authors of this book have crossed the line by insinuating that victims of crime and abuse are to blame for what happened to them, and that physiological illnesses are a direct result of negative thinking.

Personally, I think the book has a great message about positive thinking, and it is very deserving of its success. However, after reading the book, I became very paranoid of my thoughts. Again no matter how much we control our mind, it does not stop having random thoughts. A lot of thoughts are driven by fear and end up being negative. If we hear a sad story, read bad news, or watch a horrific movie, our mind reacts and creates thoughts.

As I have mentioned before, I am currently pregnant with my second child. Obviously carrying a child is a physical and emotional process, and it is a huge responsibility. Hearing stories of mothers having miscarriages and stillbirths creates anxiety within me. There have been countless moments where my mind has acted out my worst fears. I have had thoughts of losing the baby, and have imagined what it would be like to deliver a baby that has died in my uterus.

I believe that the mind creates and memorizes thought patterns that are connected to thousands of other thought patterns. This is why the mind runs rampant at such a fast pace. Before you have the chance to catch yourself, your thoughts have quickly gone to a very dark and ugly place. I feel very fortunate because I have managed to connect with my soul, and eventually my soul does interject on my mind. My soul tells my mind to stop thinking such negative thoughts, and it brings me back to a more positive frame of mind.

It goes without saying that it is not my intention to actually lose this baby. It took me years to get pregnant, and I already love this child with every inch of my being. These fear-driven, negative thoughts cannot possibly attract me to actually lose the baby, or to make my child ill. I know that God and the universe are not that abrupt, but then I get paranoid and felt so guilty about having such thoughts.

Every time I had a negative thought, I panicked and thought, *Oh no, did that negative thought just attract something negative from the universe?* I know the books say not to worry about your negative thoughts. The idea is to be conscious of your thoughts and then bring them back to a positive frequency; however, I personally found that I was spending way too much time and effort focusing on managing my thoughts. This was actually creating more stress in my life than anything else.

Throughout my spiritual journey, I have connected with my soul and I have become extremely spiritual, yet I admit that I still cannot control my thoughts. I don't think all the meditation and spirituality in the world can stop the mind from acting independently from time to time. There are some things about our existence that we cannot fully understand or control; we simply need to do our best and then submit to them. Our mind is one of those things.

It is important to be aware and conscientious about our thoughts, but spending our entire life trying to control the mind is like fighting an endless uphill battle. It is simply not worth the energy it requires. Frankly, it is counterproductive and unnecessary. We have to stop putting so much pressure on ourselves.

Thoughts are powerful, but only if you focus on them and give them power. Don't forget you, *and only you*, are in control of that power. If you have a negative thought, let it run its course, and then dismiss it with love, compassion, and ease. Know that your mind is simply processing information, and it is not your intention to manifest these negative thoughts; you do not want them to come true.

More than your thoughts, I think it is your intentions that you really have to worry about. Thoughts are random, but your intentions are not. You need to know the difference between a thought and what you intended that thought to mean. Connecting with your soul will make it easier to differentiate between the two. Once you know what your intent is, you can manifest it and bring it into your life.

Although the Law of Attraction can be used as a useful metaphor, it is not the way the universe works. I have to disagree, or at least make some amendments to this theory. I am calling my theory, which focuses on intentions rather than thoughts, the Law of Intention. As I had mentioned in chapter 7, I think that, if the universe is bringing us things, then someone or something is there making those things happen. I believe that spirit guides and angels, who work around the clock as God's helpers, manifest our intentions and fulfill our wishes. They carry out the Law of Intention.

Your spirit guides know you better than you think. They can pick up on your intent before your mind even creates a thought. If you are in a negative place in your life, you need to be particularly aware of this. If you wake up in the morning and think, *Everything is going wrong,* or, *It is going to be a horrible day,* and your intent is dark and pessimistic, then your spirit guides will bring you what you are focusing on.

Remember it is your free will to feel whatever you want to feel, and to do whatever you want to do. God and angels cannot interfere with that. We humans determine what is good and what is bad. Think about it: a $10/hr job could be a very good thing for one person, and a very bad job for a different person. Getting married and having children can be great blessings for some people, yet there are others who don't want that. How many times have you wanted something and, once you got it, you no longer saw it as a good thing. You see, there is no way God and angels can determine what is good and what is bad for people.

It is our free will to choose what we want. Again, God does not judge our free will. If you use your free will to feel sad or depressed, then that is your choice. If you choose to not ask for good things and instead focus on the things that you perceive as bad in your life, then it is your prerogative and your free will to do so.

Your spirit guides will bring you more of the same. They will give you new material, so to speak, to focus your negative thoughts on. They will continue to bring you things that make you feel sad or bad, because that is what you are intending to manifest. Before you know it, you are caught in a vicious circle. Your spirit guides and angels are probably rejoicing, as they are giving you what you want. Remember, in the spirit world, there is no distinction between good and bad. It is up to you to determine whether your intentions are good or bad for you in your life.

To be clear, a couple of random thoughts do not cause negative things to happen. However, if you are constantly focusing on all the bad things that happened in your life, and you are expending a lot of energy thinking about the fact that nothing will ever change, then your intent becomes tainted in this manner. Your intent can then come from a place of fear, anger, or self-pity.

If you apply for a job and are then instantly filled with self-doubt, and you start feeling like you're not going to get the job, then you may be telling your spirit guides that you don't really want the job. If you are in a new relationship, and you are constantly waiting for something to go wrong and for the relationship to end, then you are telling your spirit guides that you don't want this relationship, and it will eventually end. If you keep thinking you are going to get injured, you probably will get injured. You will ultimately get what you subconsciously wish for.

If someone does something to upset you, and in the heat of the moment you wish him or her ill in your mind, but you don't really intend anything bad to happen to that person, then it is okay. You had that thought out of frustration, but your intent comes from a place of love. Unfortunately, there are a lot of people that really do intend harm for others. They spend a lot of time and energy focusing on their anger and their hatred. They seek revenge and payback. They are putting negative intent onto others and out into the universe. As we will discuss in an upcoming chapter, wishing ill for others hurts you far more than anyone else.

Once again, we have free will to ask for whatever we want. Angels cannot judge what is right or wrong for you. They simply try their best to fulfill your intentions. Even though you are feeling down and asking for negative things, your angels are doing their job. They are giving you more of what you are thinking about and focusing on.

If you want good things to come to you, you have to change your intentions. You need to intend for yourself to have a good day, meet the right man or woman, and intend to forgive people who have hurt you. Most importantly you have to intend to be happy, and intend to have happy thoughts. If you intend for positive things to happen, your soul will quickly dismiss any negative thoughts that your mind creates. You don't have to worry about it so much. It will all happen naturally.

I am a pregnant mother who sometimes has negative thoughts that are driven by fear, but deep down, my intent is not tainted by fear. I know that my baby and I are blessed and taken care of. Everything is going to be fine, and I have nothing to be worried about. If something happens to this baby, I will deal with it, but I am not going to focus on that. If I allow those negative thoughts to consume me—and if I become manic, afraid, or paranoid all the time—then I may be sending my spirit guides the wrong message. I have to be careful about how much power I give to those thoughts. This is my free will and my responsibility.

Each and every single day of your life, there are many factors in play. I understand that circumstances, situations, and other people's choices often make us feel like things are out of our control. However, you must take charge and control all that you can: you can always control your free will, and you can always control your intentions. You choose how much power you give to your thoughts, and you choose how you exercise your free will.

Your upbringing, your surroundings, and your life's circumstances really have nothing to do with this. Ultimately you are responsible for your life. In order to live an authentic and meaningful life, you have to step up and assume the responsibility. You are in control of the ship of your life. Come wind, storm, sun, or calm you have to control the ship. Letting go of the wheel and blaming others only makes matters worse for you. It hinders the opportunity for you to better your life's situation. Do your part, and everything else will slowly but surely fall in place, and don't forget you have lots of help.

Like every other aspect of your spiritual journey, the first step is awareness: be aware of your intent. The second step is control: control what your intentions are. Finally, the third step is responsibility: take responsibility for the life you are creating for yourself!

Please answer the following questions. This will help you understand what you have been attracting to your life thus far. Answer the questions in order and do not read the next question until you have completed the one before:

1. What do you spend a lot of time focusing on?

2. What do you think these intentions are consequently bringing to your life?

3. How have your intentions changed over the last 10 years?

4. Yes or No. Do you often focus on the negative things that have happened in your life?
   If yes
   a. What negative things from your past are you constantly thinking about?

5. Yes or No. Have you focused on your feelings of anger or hatred for others?
   If yes
   a. Who and what for?

6. Yes or No. Do you feel sorry for yourself?

7. Yes or No. Do you feel worthy of the good things that come your way?

8. Yes or No. Do you think it's possible that your negative intentions could have brought more negative things into your life?

9. Yes or No. Do you intend on having good things happen to you?

10. Yes or No. Do you intend good things for others?

11. Yes or No. Do you think you are selfish?
    If yes
    a. Are you unnecessarily selfish at times?
    b. What experiences turned you into a selfish person?

12. Going forward, list three or four things that you wish to focus your intention on:

CHAPTER 14: CHALKBOARD IN THE SKY

In *The Education Of An Amphibian*, Aldous Huxley famously says, "We must give up the insane illusion that a conscious self, however virtuous and however intelligent, can do its work single-handed and without assistance."

It is our responsibility to live the best possible life that we can live. We owe it to God, and to God's helpers, to use them to their full potential. If you choose not to, then you are basically wasting your resources. It is like being a manager in a company with five staff to help you run the business, but not asking your staff to do anything.

If you try to do everything yourself, and you don't assign your people tasks—or follow their advice—then what is the sense of having them at your disposal? They may try to communicate with you at first, but eventually they will give up trying to help you. They will have no choice but to just be quiet and let you run your business on your own. They will have to watch you struggle and not live up to your potential.

In order for God and your spirit guides to bring you what you want, you have to ask for their guidance and their assistance. However, first you must be clear on it yourself. If you don't really know what it is that you want and don't want, then how can you expect God to bring it to you? How can we expect someone to help us, if we don't fully know what it is that we need or want?

We have already determined that our thoughts don't necessarily come true—and thank goodness for that—so we need to be clear on what exactly we intend for our lives. Right here, right now, put this book down and think about this. If you could have anything, what would you want? How would these things make your life better? Spend five minutes thinking about this.

For the majority of people, this is a very difficult question to answer and certainly not one that can be understood or clarified in one sitting. Connecting with your soul will really help you understand yourself and understand what it is that you need, and what you seek. Once you have a clear idea of how you can make your life better—and trust me you can always make your life better—then you are ready to put it into action and manifest it.

Our guardian angels can read our intent, but we can take this a step further and be more proactive in taking charge of our lives. We can assign individual tasks and jobs to our spirit guides. Imagine that there is a chalkboard in the sky, and on it you can write down everything that you want in your life. Your spirit guides can then read this imaginary *chalkboard in the sky* and help you fulfill your wishes. The spirit guides use the assistance of angels to get those tasks organized and completed.

As you progress through your life, and as your priorities change, you can wipe the chalkboard clean and assign a new set of tasks. You can do this whenever you want, and as frequently as you wish. This process of assigning tasks will also help you clarify what your intentions are for yourself, for those around you, and for the world; all these things go hand-in-hand.

The *chalkboard in the sky* can also be written out in a diary or a notebook. Actually writing these things down allows you to later come back and see how you have progressed through your life and through your spiritual journey. It is also a good way to track your growth and to get to know yourself better.

The more specific and thorough your tasks are, the more likely it will be that you get exactly what you want. If you want to find a new man or woman to spend your life with, then write it down on the *chalkboard in the sky* or in a notebook. Then below the task, in as much detail as possible, write down the traits you are looking for in your partner: tall/short, funny, humble, strong, works in public service or a business person. Whatever floats your boat—write it down.

If you want a new job, write down what type of job you intend to have. Imagine your work environment and the type of people that work with you, and then write it down. What kind of boss would you like? What type of pay do you expect? If you are dreaming about a new house, picture every nook and cranny of the house. Whatever tasks you assign, make them clear with as much detail as possible.

In this manner you can create and manifest the life that you want and deserve. This is your life! You are not helpless, and you are certainly not out of control. You are in charge of your life, and you can manifest any-thing to happen in it. Nothing is impossible, and nothing is too big to ask for. Give the responsibility to your guardian angels, have faith that it will be handled, and then just surrender. Surrendering is a very important part of the process.

When I first started trying to manifest my intentions, by communicating with my spirit guides and assigning tasks, I did it every single day non-stop. Every day in my mind, I would repeat and remind my spirit guides of what I wanted and what I needed. I would pray, I would ask, I would put it on the chalkboard in the sky over and over again. I thought that, because I am strong willed, I will be able to manifest what I am asking for faster by continuously focusing on the same things. Let me tell you, this is simply exhausting, unnecessary, and frankly counterproductive.

I have heard and read a lot about the concept of asking and praying. Many spiritual leaders say that asking for things actually pushes the things you want away from you. After many years of confusion, I think I finally understand what they mean. From my understanding, when we pray for things and ask God or the angels to bring us things, the actual act and emotions associated with *asking* creates a *want*. This emotion of *wanting* and *needing* dominates our energy in a negative way. It no longer becomes about the thing you were asking for. The *need* and *want* take over.

If you want something so badly, and you focus all you have on it, and then it doesn't happen immediately, your mind starts to create doubt and fear. You start to think that it is not going happen.

For example, like most families my family has been impacted by the economy. Being self-employed is a little risky when you have a mortgage, a family, and a baby on the way. I started to manifest a full-time job for myself and for my husband. I focused on it so much that, when we didn't get the first few jobs we applied for, I started to worry. I would lay awake at night thinking and praying, *If we don't get jobs soon then our savings will run out. What if we can't pay our mortgage, or afford to send our son to his Montessori preschool next year?* I then followed those thoughts with, *Oh please, angels, bring us jobs and financial security otherwise we will be in trouble.*

I did not realize it at the time, but my intent was completely coming from a place of fear, and fear is a negative intent. This was another aha moment for me. You cannot ask, pray, or assign tasks and then immediately have doubt or fear. It's not all black and white, and it's not easy to understand. For your own sanity, just surrender and have faith.

If this had happened to me a few years ago, before I went on my spiritual journey, I would have given up and stopped having faith. If I didn't get what I was asking for, I would have stopped believing in spirit guides and angels, and I would have wallowed in self-pity.

As I am writing these sentences, I am actually having another epiphany at this very moment—by asking for a full-time job, I have been sending mixed messages to my guardian angels. My request for a job was conflicting with other things that I intended to do in my life. It has always been my intention to become more spiritual. I want to make a difference in the world, and I felt that writing a book was one way of accomplishing this. I had put all these tasks on my chalkboard in the sky some time ago.

I applied for jobs and didn't get a single interview, so I decided to take the time to continue on my spiritual journey and to start writing. I now realize that it would have been extremely difficult for me to work full-time and write this book, as I am having a difficult pregnancy. My husband is home, and he helps out with my three-year-old son, so I can concentrate on this book project. If we had both gotten full-time jobs, I would not have started writing. Once I have the baby, this book project would have been pushed at least a few years into the future, and who knows where I will be then.

I thought God was not listening to me and was ignoring my requests, but without even realizing it, my spirit guides helped me manifest one of my wishes. Not getting a full-time job may have been a blessing after all. I am writing this book; I have picked up some work, and I am surrendering my financial obligations to God and my spirit guides. I have faith that I will be taken care of.

You should never judge events or non-events in your life as let downs or disappointments. As humans we cannot see the whole picture, and we do not have the capability to understand why certain things happen and why others do not. This is what ultimately makes life so fun and exciting, so enjoy the unpredictable nature of your life. Don't get stuck in your ways, and don't get too comfortable in your routine because you don't know when things will change. Instead of fearing and dreading change, prepare for it and accept it. Take enjoyment in not knowing what will happen tomorrow. Become a little more spontaneous in your nature. Again, I love the saying: "nothing is good or bad, but thinking makes it so."

If you are let go from your job, it doesn't necessarily mean that it is a punishment from the universe. Maybe the angels are giving you some time to reflect on yourself and what you want out of life because you have been intending to do that. Perhaps you were not truly fulfilled at that job, and subconsciously you were wishing for a change but were too afraid to quit.

If money or material possessions are taken away from you, maybe it is because deep down your intention is to find pure happiness—the type that money can't buy. The material things in your life may be putting you in a state of material-comatose and causing you more harm than progress. Perhaps by taking away your possessions, your spirit guides are helping you reach some of your other, more meaningful goals.

If you apply for a job or a promotion and don't get it, then perhaps that job is not meant to be. There may be something bigger and better coming for you. Maybe you will meet the man or the woman of your dreams, or have the perfect boss at your next job. You just have to be patient and wait a little while for all the stars to align, so to speak.

Remember other people's free will is also in play. You may want something, and your spirit guides may want to give it to you, but they cannot interfere with someone else's free will. If a boss wants to fire you, an interviewer doesn't want to hire you, or if a man or woman doesn't want to date you, then God's helpers cannot interfere and change their choice to do so.

Rest assured though, where one door closes, another door or window opens. It is your spirit guides and angels that are opening those doors and windows for you. They are divinely orchestrating your future every single moment of every single day. The paths may be constantly changing, but the end destination will be what you are asking for. Every single one of us is always being taken care of, even if we cannot see it in the present moment.

You acquire what you want by writing it on your chalkboard in the sky and then you surrender by imagining you already have it. If you imagine you already have what you want then you do not create a *want*. Instead you create the emotion of *gratitude*. In this manner, you are praying and asking from a place of love and thankfulness. In your mind's reality it has already happened, and therefore, it will happen.

If you are asking for money, imagine your debt is all paid off and your bank account has money in it. Thank God and the angels for sending you money and alleviating your debt. If you are asking for a job, imagine you already have your dream job and now you are simply waiting for the start date.

Your chalkboard in the sky can also be used to help others. Although everyone has their own spirit guides and angels, we can always send some extra love and some extra help. As a parent, you can ask one or two of your spirit guides to stay with your child. Ask them to protect him or her while he or she is at school or at a sleepover. If someone you love is on the wrong path or at risk of being in danger, you can send your spirit guides and angels to help them. Your spirit guides work with their spirit guides and become more powerful. Think of it like pooling your resources.

From a young age whenever I saw an ambulance, police cars, or a fire truck zoom past me, with sirens blasting, I always said a quick prayer and hoped everything would be fine. Since I have started communicating with my spirit guides and angels, I now assign a task. I ask the angels to head immediately to the scene to see if they can do something to diffuse a situation, to heal someone who is wounded, or help put out a fire.

When I used to hear that a child had gone missing on the news or that a dangerous killer was on the loose, I felt so helpless. While driving at night, I would often see people stuck on the side of the road or someone trying to hitchhike. Although I wanted to help that complete stranger, I knew it was not safe for me to do so, especially if my son was with me. I would drive by feeling sorry and guilty for not stopping.

Now I ask the angels to see if they can do something to help. I assign a task and put it on the chalkboard in the sky. So many times I check back and the missing child has been found, the fugitive has been caught, or someone else picked up the hitchhiker. I obviously don't know if my prayer helped the situation, but it might have. I feel good because at least I tried to do something to help. By assigning tasks and asking for help, I no longer feel helpless, and this has empowered me to try and make a difference as often as I can.

Remember we all have our own free will, and God and his or her helpers cannot interfere until someone asks. By assigning tasks, you are asking and exercising your free will. You are asking for yourself, and you are asking on behalf of others. I believe a lot of people in the world are already doing this. If we all start asking for help and protecting one another, we can make the world a better place. When many people send prayer, love, light, angels—which are all essentially the same thing—to the same place, powerful things happen. An immeasurably strong army shows up from the spirit world in order to serve, protect, and heal.

Obviously there is no scientific evidence or concrete proof that spirit guides and angels exist. There is also no evidence that God exists. However, if you stop, sense, and connect with them, you will feel them. You will experience them. You may physically feel them as a slight vibration or tingling on your skin, or you may simply feel their presence around you.

When you acknowledge their existence and communicate with them, I guarantee you will never feel alone again. You have a permanent posse or entourage that stays with you at all times, no matter where you are, or where you go. They walk beside you; they hold your hand during difficult times; they laugh with you, and they cry with you. Feel them, and allow them to empower you. Face the hardships and challenges in your life, and know that you have all the support and guidance you need.

Image the blank space below as your chalkboard in the sky. Write down what you want on it. Suppose you have five guardian angels. Assign each one of them a task, and describe the task in as much detail as possible:

CHAPTER 15: ENERGY EQUILIBRIUM

As we continue to peal the layers of our onion from the inside out and dig deeper into our spiritual journey, we need to clarify and understand the important concept of universal energy. Energy exists within us, and it exists all around us. It is simple science. Energy is the central idea in both classic physics and quantum physics.

Technically there are two uses of the word ‘*energy*’ that are often mistaken for a single concept. Scientists define *energy* as an indirectly observed quantity in physics. It is often understood as the ability a physical system has to do work on another physical system. On the other hand, energy is also understood in a metaphysical or spiritual way.

Speaking about a person's energy is a metaphysical concept. When energy is a representation of the potential to do work, it is a scientific concept. However, I think that the two different meanings of the word energy go hand in hand. One person's energy has the ability to do work on or impact another person's energy.

We don't need to view scientific research and evidence to know that energy exists. You can be facing one direction, with headphones on, and someone can silently walk up behind you, and you will be able to sense them. What you are sensing is their energy. Some people can walk into a place and, without saying a word, light up the room. They instantly make people feel relaxed and comfortable. On the other hand, some people walk into a room and, without saying or doing a thing, make people feel awkward and/or uneasy. This happens because each one of us carries our own specific energy, which goes with us everywhere we go.

Energy exists inside of us, and it is emitted from within our body. Once released, it sits and radiates on the outside of our skin. It circles the body like a giant vertical halo and is commonly referred to as a person's aura. Scientifically, the aura is called the human energy field (HEF). Every single human being and living organism on this planet has an aura around them. The notion of the aura and the human energy field is by no means a new concept.

In the mid-19th century the notable chemist, geologist, and philosopher Baron Carl Ludwig von Reichenbach dedicated his last years to studying and experimenting this energy. He called this vital energy or life force the 'odic force' and concluded that it permeates all plants, animals, and humans. Reichenbach also said that the odic force had a positive and negative flux. The energy had a dark and a light side, and individuals were able to emanate it. In their book *Future Science: Life Energies and the Physics of Paranormal Phenomena*, John White and Stanley Krippner stated that they found references to the aura, or the human energy field, in 97 different cultures.

Many experts have concluded that a person can have either a healthy or an unhealthy effect on someone else by simply being present. One person's aura can be either pleasant or jarring for another person. Some energy is nurturing, and some energy is draining. Depending on your mood, your aura can be bright, positive, and inviting, or it can be dark, negative, and repelling. This is why some people make us instantly feel comfortable, at ease, and even happy. This is also the reason why we simply can't stand to be around other people.

Believe it or not, energy affects human interaction and our individual relationships on a non-verbal non-physical level. Our energy communicates with other people without our knowledge and without our active participation. This happens on a level that is out of our direct control, basically on a subconscious level. After spending a lot of time thinking about how energy works and how it pertains to our existence, I believe there is such a thing as an energy balance in the world: all the energy in the world wants to be in balance.

Human energy has an innate need to be equal to the energies that surrounds it, or with which it comes into contact. Its constant goal is to be in equilibrium with the energy fields around it. In other words, our energy wants to be in balance with the energy of the people around us. This is possible because human energy fields have a magnetic effect, which automatically communicates and draws energy from other human energy fields and auras. I call this the *energy equilibrium*.

Positive people, with strong, clean auras, have extra energy stored up. Negative people, with dark weak auras, have a depleted energy field, and they are constantly in need of positive energy. When different types of energies—different types of people—come into contact with each other, their energies try to balance each other by coming to a common ground. Negative energy automatically draws positive energy from other energy fields. Negative people unintentionally draw energy from positive people. This is why some people are capable of sucking the energy out of a room and can single-handedly change the mood of a group.

You may have noticed, from your past experiences, that when you start spending a lot of time with a friend or a family member who is going through rough patch in life, and is often sad or pessimistic, that it eventually rubs off on you. On the flip side, if you have people around you who, even during difficult times, maintain an optimistic outlook and stay positive, they consequently inspire you and lift your spirits. I believe this happens because, without your knowledge, their energy impacts your energy.

There have been many studies conducted suggesting that, if you hang around divorced people, you are more likely to get divorced yourself. If your close friends or family members are obese, you are more likely to overeat and gain weight. If you hang out with people who have a pessimistic outlook on life, you are more likely to have a pessimistic attitude. If you have rich successful people in your social circle, you are more likely to succeed. If this happens to some people, I think that these situations are impacted by the *energy equilibrium*.

Also I believe that the Law of Attraction works for the human energy field: like attracts like. Positive people, with bright auras, are attracted to other positive people. Similarly negative people, with dark auras, ultimately find other negative people like themselves. This can again be explained by my theory of *energy equilibrium*. It is easier for energy to reach equilibrium among people with comparable auras.

This is why, in society, we have groups or families that are all similar in attitude, and similar in the way they approach their lives. Some families and/or groups of people lift each other up, support each other, and enhance each other's quality of life. This is also perhaps why dysfunction and constant heartache exists within other families and/or groups. Because we keep attracting people who have similar auras to our own, it is very important to not get dragged down in a rut and to increase our energy levels. I will talk about this in a lot more detail in the upcoming chapters.

Although the *energy equilibrium* is in constant motion on a level that is non-verbal and non-physical—in terms of our conscious everyday human interaction—we do control some aspects of it. Humans control the type of energy they create. I think we have the ability to create different types of energy, and this is why we must take responsibility for our individual energy.

Our thoughts, feelings, emotions, and actions create energy. I am not talking about the random thoughts that our mind processes. As we have already discussed, both positive and negative random thoughts can be quickly silenced and discarded by the soul. I am talking about the thoughts that we focus on and turn into our intentions. I am talking about the thoughts that create feelings, which are emitted through our emotions and our actions.

Negative intentions, feelings, and emotions are dangerous; however, I believe actions create even more potent amounts of energy. Gossiping, backstabbing, criticizing, or hurting people produces negative energy. When you fight with people, attack them, or verbally or physically abuse them, you are responsible for engaging in situations that create masses of negative energy.

Albert Einstein proved that energy never dies. He also concluded that energy cannot be created or destroyed. According to the Law of

Conservation of Energy, which is a law of physics, "The total amount of energy in a system remains constant over time." The law states that energy can only be transformed from one state to another, and that the total sum of the energy that exists in the universe does not change. Therefore, technically speaking, energy exists within us all and we transform it into either positive energy or negative energy. Scientific laws are complicated and require long complex explanations. There has been an enormous amount of research and studies done on energy in both classic and quantum physics, to which you can refer.

Although physics can be used to understand and define many aspects of spirituality, I am intentionally not going to confuse my message by backing it with research and findings. I am talking about energy in terms that make sense to me. This understanding came to me during my spiritual journey. To say that, "someone is creating negative energy," has become a common statement that is widely accepted. Therefore, I am going to continue to use the term *created*, with the understanding that in actuality the energy is being transformed from one state to another.

Oprah Winfrey has often spoken about energy on the Oprah Winfrey show. She loves to reference a dialogue delivered by actress Whoopi Goldberg in the movie *The Color Purple* where she says, "Everything you done to me, already done to you." Oprah often teaches people that whatever you do to others has already been done to you, so be careful of your actions.

People often say things like, "What goes around comes around," and, "You reap what you sow," and my favorite one is, "The universe is a bigger bitch than you'll ever be." All these sayings refer to the fact that your intentions and actions have consequences that will inevitably affect you. It is a great message, but I wanted to get to the bottom of how this works exactly. How do our intentions and actions literally affect our own lives, and the lives of those around us?

I believe that emotions such as anger, hatred, jealousy, worry, and fear all create negative energy. When you wish ill upon someone, or if you focus your intentions on being angry or revengeful towards someone, you create various amounts of energy. When you experience these types of negative thoughts and emotions, you create negative energy within yourself.

This negative energy is created inside of your body, and when it is released—through your feelings, emotions, and actions—first and foremost the energy must pass through your own aura, or human energy field, before it can find its way to the person you have intended it for. As energy moves it loses its intensity. As it passes through various energy fields, it becomes more and more diluted. Therefore, you get the strongest dose of the energy that you create. All of the anger, hatred, and/or revenge you wish upon someone else, affects you far more than anyone else.

Energy is not static—it is constantly in motion—and aside from impacting human energy fields, it also impacts surrounding spaces. Once energy has crossed through a human energy field, it sticks to surroundings: to homes, to work spaces, and to places of social gatherings. Therefore, the energy you create not only impacts your aura, but it remains in the places where you live, and subsequently it may impact your family, friends, and acquaintances.

In places where a lot of crying, yelling, arguing, and dysfunction occur, negative stale energy builds up and infiltrates onto the walls and the corners of that space. As soon as you walk into that place you can subconsciously feel the dull, draining, and uncomfortable negative energy. Similarly in places where love, support, peace, and laughter exist, positive energy builds up and vibrates on the walls. One feels re-energized, safe, and calm when they walk into those types of rooms. This is why it feels so good to be in spas, places of worship, and/or religious institutions.

This following recaps the way I think energy works:

1. The person creating the energy gets the strongest dose of that energy, and they are impacted by it the most. The majority of that energy sticks to that person's aura.

2. After energy passes through the creator's energy field, it then must pass through the walls that surround it.

3. Some energy sticks to the creator's home or to the surroundings where they emitted the energy.

4. As a result of passing through the creator's human energy field and through his or her surroundings, the majority of the energy is left behind; therefore the original energy becomes weaker and less potent.

5. A diluted version of that energy then makes its way to find the person or people for which the energy was originally intended.

6. That energy then passes through their energy fields and sticks to their aura.

7. The energy moves through his or her aura, and as it passes through his or her surroundings, some of the energy stays behind and binds itself to the walls, corners, and doors of their living space.

8. The energy does not stop there. The kinetic energy keeps moving.

9. The energy is finally emitted into a large shared pool, where it impacts the world and the entire global society.

I firmly believe that this outlines why the world is in its current global situation. On a daily basis, millions of people emit an astronomical amount of negative energy into the world. Humans have been negatively impacting their own lives, the lives of the people around them, and the lives of every living being on this planet for centuries. With each passing generation, this negative energy just keeps compounding and multiplying. Sadly we continue to create negative energy and overwhelm our world and our universe.

At some point or another everyone asks themselves the question, *How can I help change the world*? I think the answer is very simple—you can individually change the world by individually creating some much-needed positive energy. Positive energy is much more powerful than negative energy. It is capable of neutralizing and combusting the negative energy that exists in our human energy fields, in our surroundings, and in our global energy pool. Small amounts of positive energy can destroy astronomical amounts of negative energy.

The simplest way to create positive energy is through love. Love is the strongest energy in the world. Smiling, laughing, hugging, caring, and sharing are all forms of love. When they are felt and expressed they create positive energy. Praying, meditating, and connecting with your spiritual self also comes from a place of love, and it also produces positive energy. This energy is a thousand times stronger than any form of negative energy. I will say it again: love is the strongest energy in the world!

Small amounts of positive energy, created through love, can instantly destroy or transform unimaginable amounts of negative energy. Going back to my analogy of the onion, and peeling the layers from the inside out, love also must be passed from the inside out. You must first love yourself, before you are able to truly love others.

By focusing on loving and compassionate thoughts, you inadvertently help yourself and the people around you and you also help heal the world. First and foremost, the positive energy that you create will penetrate your own human energy field and aura. Through the Law of Attraction, your positive energy will attract other positive people and bring them to your life, and this will better your life's experience. The positive energy will stick to your surroundings and make your home and work area a calm peaceful place to live your life.

This same energy will then bring beautiful, positive things to the people for whom you intend that love. Your positive energy will combust any negative energy that may be trapped inside of their human energy fields. It will also make their homes and their surrounding better. Eventually the positive energy that you created and set into motion will eventually make its way out into the world. It will help destroy the negative energy that is currently dominating the world.

Again, actions create much more powerful energies than intentions, feelings, and emotions, so use this to your advantage. This is why good deeds, volunteering, and doing charity work is so important. Giving your time and money to help others is a wonderful way to create heaps of positive energy. Good deeds can be as simple as opening the door for someone and giving them a smile. It can be helping an elderly person across the street, assisting someone in a time of need, or showing compassion for someone who has made a mistake.

If just half the people on this planet start to create some form of positive energy every single day, imagine the possibilities. We could neutralize and destroy all the negative energy, which has such a strong hold on our world. We could create a global pool of positive energy, from which anyone in need could draw from. It would make our individual lives so much more calm and pleasant that we would have fewer conflicts with others, and our planet would start to heal.

In previous chapters, I have repeatedly said that we need to increase our awareness, gain control, and accept responsibility for our lives. In this same manner, each one of us has to be aware of our energy; we need to try and control it, and also take responsibility for the type of energy we are creating, emitting, and spreading. Do it for yourself, and do it for the world.

There is one other aspect of energy I'd like to discuss; it is in correlation to fear. As someone who spent many years inundated by fear, I really started to think about the concept of fear and how it works. My first realization about fear is that it works in two completely different contexts.

Most people experience fear as an emotion. As I mentioned in Chapter 2, to different extents most people are inundated by the emotion of fear. Like I said, fear is a dominating emotion that is created by the mind's ego; thus, it is a false emotion that traps people in either the past or the future. Fear does not exist in one's soul. By living in the moment one can start to separate the ego from the mind and reconnect with the soul; therefore, eliminate the stronghold of fear.

Fear has another, very different, purpose that goes way back to evolution. Fear is an animal instinct, which has the ability to sense danger. It is a survival mechanism; it creates an urge to either confront or flee a situation. Many famous psychologist including Robert Plutchik and John B. Watson suggest that fear is one of the few basic or innate emotions that exist within humans.

This really got me thinking. If fear does not exist in the soul, and if it is a figment of the ego driven mind's imagination, then how can fear be a legitimate emotion? Emotions can only be created either through the soul's guidance or from the ego's guidance. Therefore, fear as an animal instinct cannot be an emotion.

I understand that I am going against what psychologists have been saying for decades; however, logic leads me to see things differently. So where does fear come from and why? I think that fear is not an emotion; rather it is a physical response to the *energy equilibrium*.

It is an innate instinct and a survival mechanism, which takes its lead from our energy. When someone comes into your energy who is intending to harm you, his or her negative intentions create immense negative energy. Because of the *energy equilibrium* your energy wants to be equal to the energies around you. However, when extremely negative energy enters your auric field, it cannot possibly balance with your energy. Your energy then communicates this to you by setting off all sorts of warning signs on the mind, body, and soul level.

Physically your heart may start to beat faster, and/or the hair on the back of your neck may stand up. Your energy will sound off an alarm to your soul that you are in danger. Your soul then kicks your intuition into high gear, which will likely give you an uneasy feeling of knowing that something is not quite right.

Reportedly, the majority of people who have been attacked have all said that they had experienced these warning signs; however, they chose to ignore them. This in turn gave their attacker the opportunity to take advantage of them. Many victims say they did so because they didn't want to be rude. Society taught them to be nice and to always give people the benefit of the doubt. I'm sure a Zebra never sees a lion coming and thinks, *Maybe he's just coming to say hi. Perhaps he won't eat me; I really should give him the benefit of the doubt.* You better believe the zebra is going to run for his life and would never chance it!

Emotional fear is false and baseless. Fear driven by the *energy equilibrium* is very real and should be taken very seriously. Unfortunately people with negative intentions do exist in the world, and we can find ourselves in situations where we can be harmed. However, you don't need to spend your life worrying about when or where this may happen. Your energy is doing all this work for you, 24 hours a day and 7 days a week, so you don't have to. The only thing you need to remember is, if and when warning signs of fear come over you, take action and get yourself as far away from the situation or individual as possible.

I'd like you to start thinking about energy by answering the following questions. Energy is a crucial part of understanding your life's experience, so please do not skip over these questions.

1.   Do you think you are a positive person or a negative person?

2. What do people who do not know you usually say about you?

3. What type of first impression do you usually make? (Do people seem to like you off the bat, or does it take time for people to warm up to you?)

4. Yes or No. Are you are a person who drains positive energy from other people?

5. Do certain people in your life drain your positive energy? If yes.
    a. Do you think these people consequently have a negative impact on your life?

    b. Who are these people?

6. Yes or No. Do you sense that you sometimes make others feel uncomfortable?
    If yes
    a. Do you think this could be a response to your energy?

7. List all the ways you create negative energy (Fighting, yelling, manipulation):

8. List all the ways you create positive energy (Loving, laughing, helping):

9. Are you mainly creating positive energy or negative energy?

CHAPTER 16: IDENTIFY YOUR ENERGY

Through your feelings, emotions, intentions, and actions, the goal is to create as little negative energy as possible and to create as much positive energy as you can. Try to be forgiving, happy, and optimistic. Try to be patient, cooperative, and non-judgmental. Try not to let little things bother you. Try not to spread your negative energy and create unnecessary drama, and certainly avoid getting into verbal or physical altercations.

Although, let's face it, life is complicated and at times difficult. As a result, we all create both positive and negative energy to different degrees. It is a healthy and normal part of life. However, it is how we deal with our energy, and with the energy of others, that matters the most.

Different people create and exert energy to different extents. Also different people handle themselves and their energy differently. Over time people get into certain habits, or behave in certain ways, which affect their energy and their lives. This is a byproduct of their upbringing, surroundings, and individual personalities. There are three major groups of people whose energy types I would like to identify and discuss. These specific energy types are the ones we need to particularly understand because they seriously impact lives, relationships, and our global society.

1. THE ROLLER COASTER ENERGY

We all know people who are exceptionally powerful, high energy, fun people. Unfortunately these people have a tough time sustaining their positive energy; they often have a quiet, gloomy, and negative side to them also. Depending on their mood, sometimes they are on a high and sometimes they are on a low. This is why I call this type of person a *Roller Coaster Energy*.

The problem with individuals who have a lot of mood swings is that, along with their emotional states, their energy also drastically spikes and dips. These people exert their energy at a much more rapid speed than others, essentially because they have very powerful and dominating human energy fields. Unknowingly they can release strong doses of positive energy in a short period of time. In the same manner, without saying or doing much, they are capable of quickly releasing incredibly strong potent amounts of negative energy also.

On a good day, these people can walk into a room and command it. They are the life of the party. Their energy is bright and positive as they laugh, are energetic, and have fun. People love to be around them because, by simply being in their presence, their own energy is lifted. However, when their mood is altered and they are feeling down, the same person's energy becomes dark, gloomy, and pessimistic.

He or she may think that by being quiet or disconnected they are not bothering anyone else, but their negative energy most certainly affects the people around them. Because of the energy equilibrium, their negative energy balances itself by draining the positive energy from the people around them. They are literally capable of sucking the energy out of a room.

The consequence of being a *Roller Coaster Energy* is that people don't know what to expect from you. When around you, your acquaintances and loved ones may feel like they are walking on eggshells. Sometimes your positive energy revitalizes them, and sometimes your negative energy drains them. They don't know what type of energy you will bring on any given day, so they will never truly be comfortable around you. They will also have difficulty getting to know the real you. They may love the fun loving carefree side of you, but dislike the quiet, pessimistic, and moody side of you. Needless to say this can cause a lot of tension and problems within your relationships.

Everyone is allowed to have a bad day, and feel down or ill from time to time. No one should feel like they have to put on an act or pretend to be happy all the time—this is not what I am talking about. It takes a lot more than a bad day or two to impact your energy and your aura. I am asking you to simply be aware of your energy, and for you to acknowledge the way it impacts the people around you. This will definitely help you take responsibility for the types of relationships you have in your life. It will also help you understand why people respond to you the way that they do.

If you identify yourself as a *Roller Coaster Energy*, the advice I can give is for you to get off the ride, and stop being this way. Try to become more consistent with your mood and your energy. Instead of exerting all of your positive energy at a single party or event, learn to control and preserve your energy.

How do you control your energy? I know it sounds too easy, but again by simply being aware of your mood and your energy, you will have the strength and the ability to control it. Look around, and be aware of how people are reacting to you. If you are in a bad mood or are feeling down, look around, and check to see if people are quiet or uncomfortable around you. If you sense that they are, then perhaps put a smile on your face or show people a small part of your fun party side. You don't have to put on an act or be the life of the party, but neutralize the situation.

If you are feeling incredibly low and unable to force a smile, then be honest with the people around you. Come clean and tell them how you are feeling. Take responsibility for impacting the energy and the mood of the group. If that doesn't help lift your spirits, then perhaps remove yourself from the situation, and give yourself a time-out. During your time-out, you can take a walk or do what you need to do in order to clear your head.

Pushing your feelings aside, feeling guilty, or being hard on yourself will only make the problem worse. Allow yourself a moment to feel and to understand why you are feeling the way you are. Give yourself the time to sort through the emotions you are experiencing. Try to figure out the source of the problem or the root cause of your mood. This way you can deal with the greater issue at hand and prevent it from happening again.

Think about it, feel the emotion, accept it, and then let it pass with love and compassion.

Breathing, exercising, and meditation can be great ways to calm and control your energy. Also connecting with your soul and understanding who you are may spiritually help you deal with some of your internal problems. Being at peace with your internal conflicts and issues will bring clarity and calmness to your life. This will consequently help you control your moods and your energy.

2. THE GO-TO ENERGY

The second type of energy I want to identify is people with *Go-To Energy*. There are many very rational, positive people that automatically become the *go-to* person for their family, friends, and co-workers. People are naturally drawn to them and feel comfortable confiding in them. Without saying or doing a whole lot, they make people feel better. I think that I am one of these people.

Obviously, we all need to share and discuss our feelings with one another, and this is a healthy process; however, the *Go-To Energy* deals with a lot of people who are constantly talking about their own problems, conflicts, and relationships. In this situation, one person is doing all of the talking and emotional releasing, while the other person is doing all of the listening, absorbing, comforting and supporting. It is not a two way dialogue or discussion.

I have spoken to many people who are a *Go-To Energy* type, who like myself, spend a lot of time consoling others and listening to their problems. I found one common problem amongst people with this type of energy: deep down these people are sad, drained, and in certain cases even depressed. The worst part is that, most often, they have no idea why.

Like everyone else, they have problems of their own, but those problems do not equate to their emotional state. They know that their problems should not make them feel as sad as they do, but they can't help it. It is understandable for one to experience sadness and/or depression if he or she has had a rough childhood, a difficult upbringing, or has suffered through a traumatic loss or event; however, a *Go-To Energy* often experiences similar sentiments without having anything all that serious or traumatic happen to them. This causes a lot of confusion and frustration within them. I can personally relate to this.

Originally I thought that constantly seeing other people's problems, listening to their sad stories, and witnessing their pain naturally made a person sad. It is difficult to keep people's secrets and to have empathy for their situations without turning your own emotions into sympathy. When you cannot intervene or change someone's circumstances, you are naturally left feeling very helpless. I thought this is what caused sadness in a *Go-To Energy* type. However, I now realize that there is a lot more to it than this.

As we discussed earlier, positive people have extra stored up energy. Focusing one's intent on sentiments such as anger, jealousy, fear, and revenge creates negative energy. People who are going through problems are likely focusing on at least one of these emotions, and as a result, have created negative energy to some extent. These people are feeling down and blue because they desperately need to release the negative energy that they have bottled up inside their bodies. They may also have been involved in a fight or a verbal altercation, which consequently created and emitted potent amounts of negative energy into their own human energy field and aura. They may be in dire need of some positive energy to neutralize and destroy that negative energy.

Because they are unaware of how to create some positive energy for themselves, they seek it from an external source, which is most often their go-to person. Essentially, people bring their unhealthy negative energy to their go-to person because they are drawn to that person's strong, bright, healthy positive energy. While confiding in a *Go-To Energy*, crying on his or her shoulder, gossiping about someone and/or expressing what's on their mind, they release their pent up negative energy. They physically and emotionally feel a lot better because they simultaneously take some of the listener's positive energy. In this manner they recharge their own batteries, so to speak.

The listener, the Go-To Energy, is left feeling sad and drained because someone else's negative energy has been passed onto them. Not only that, positive energy has been taken from their human energy field. By the time they destroy that person's negative energy by creating more positive energy—through thoughts, emotions, and actions that come from love—someone else comes around and takes their positive energy again, and leaves them with more negative energy to deal with. Unknowingly this happens again and again and again to the Go-To Energy, and over time, it takes a serious toll on them emotionally and physically.

I know this woman who is a wonderful mother with many children. She has a large family, and works as a manager in a large department store. As we were talking one day, she told me that everyone always comes to her with their problems. At work all the women come and tell her about the fights and conflicts they are having. Also her family and friends are constantly confiding in her. She is the go-to person in every aspect of her life. When I asked her how she handles this, she said she was fine. She expressed that she enjoys listening to people, and likes to comfort and support her loved ones.

In a separate conversation, one day we were talking about our feelings and emotions, and about how rough life is sometimes. She admitted that she often comes home and cries at the end of the day. Sometimes she said she cries, and cries, and cries for no reason at all. She added that she constantly feels drained and has spent years being depressed and even suicidal. At the time, neither of us linked her Go-To Energy type to her feelings of sadness and depression.

It now makes perfect sense as to why this woman feels this way. At home, at work, and in her social circle people are constantly draining this woman's positive energy, and leaving their negative energy behind for her to deal with. She literally takes on people's problems, and then she spends time worrying about them. Worrying is yet another emotion that creates negative energy.

This was another big realization for me. By worrying about other people, you create and release negative energy, which strongly impacts your own human energy field. Instead of helping that person, your worry creates negative energy, which eventually makes its way, from your aura and surroundings, into their aura and their surroundings. Worrying unintentionally makes matters worse for you and for your loved ones.

As a result, this woman has to physically cry in order to release the negative energy that keeps wedging itself onto her aura. This poor woman is confused because she doesn't understand why she feels the need to cry and feel so sad. It is understandable how all this confusion—not to mention the spikes and drops in her energy—can eventually lead to depression and suicidal thoughts.

As I had mentioned before, I used to work as a manager in a luxury jewelry store, where I managed a staff of 15. Because sales commissions were high and the environment was fast-paced and stressful, I witnessed a very dark side of human nature at that job. Individually they were all wonderful people, but as a group, they were constantly fighting, gossiping, backstabbing, and getting back at one another.

Several times a week, I would walk into the store and instantaneously someone would approach me and start telling me about a conflict they are having with another staff member; I wouldn't even get a chance to put my jacket or purse down. I would take that person into my office to hear them out. I had a see-through glass door, and right away I would see one or two other people standing outside my door waiting to tell me their side of the story.

I gained so much experience resolving staff problems, that I pretty much have a PhD in conflict resolution. Although the problems seldom involved me personally, constantly being around fighting and listening to issues really affected me. At the time I was also having trouble conceiving; I couldn't get pregnant. My doctor told me that stress was probably a contributing factor and that, if I wanted to have children, I needed to eliminate it.

Luckily a voice inside me told me to take myself out of that situation and to quit the job. After I quit, I took two small vacations and got pregnant within two months. I now understand that my stress was probably caused by being around so much negative energy all the time, and by constantly being drained of my positive energy.

Go-To Energy types are natural givers, so it is difficult for me to tell myself, let alone anyone else, to stop helping others and to start taking care of number one; however, it is important to take care of yourself. It is vital that you protect your own energy. You are no good to anyone else if you are feeling sad, unhappy, and drained. Keep in mind that in order to have true compassion, empathy, and love for others, you must first have it for yourself.

You also need someone to talk to and to share your problems with. Make sure you are not keeping things bottled up inside. Confide in the people that confide in you. After hearing someone out, lean on them and tell them how you are feeling. These types of conversations and relationships allow for great energy exchanges. Like a teeter-totter, you will balance each other. You will both leave the conversation feeling comforted, supported, and happier.

If you are constantly submerged in a negative environment that you cannot control or change, then perhaps you need to re-evaluate how important it is for you to be there. For the situations that you cannot avoid and don't want to avoid, you simply need to take steps in order to protect your human energy field and your aura. You can call upon your spirit guides and the angels to stop someone from taking your positive energy; also ask them to take the negative energy that people are releasing onto you and immediately destroy it with the positive energy that already exists in the universe.

As soon as a person starts talking about their problems with you, or if you feel negative energy around you, quickly assign a task and put it on the chalkboard in the sky. Your spirit guides and angels will take care of it. You can also protect yourself by wrapping yourself in white light. I will explain the concept of wrapping yourself in light and protecting your aura in the next chapter.

3. THE TRAPPED ENERGY

Lastly, the third type of energy I want to identify is people who are a *Trapped Energy*. These are the people who keep everything bottled up inside. They do not like to express their feelings or their emotions in front of others, not even their loved ones. People rarely see them cry, communicate their sentiments, or express any type of deep emotion.

They are typically uncomfortable with being vulnerable in front of people, or they feel so bad about burdening others with their problems that they simply don't. If they are angry, upset, or have a conflict with someone they internalize it and keep it to themselves. Because they keep every negative thought, feeling, and emotion pent up, their negative energy becomes trapped inside of their bodies. They then struggle to find ways to release it.

People who are a *Trapped Energy* type can be perceived by the outside world a few different ways. Sometimes they can be generalized as harsh and insensitive people. Men are often Trapped Energy types. Historically and culturally, from a young age, men are raised to be tough and strong. They are taught that boys don't cry and should not show emotion. The older they get, the more these men internalize these expectations and keep their feelings to themselves.

In many cases men are perhaps even more sensitive than women, but you would never know it because they work hard to hide their emotions. They then act out in ways that woman do not understand. Instead of coming out and saying what is bothering them, they may appear angry or in a foul mood for no obvious reason. They may pick a fight or get upset about a completely unrelated issue. What they say does not correlate to how they behave. This confuses and frustrates the people in their lives.

This type of energy, however, is not gender specific; many women are considered insensitive too. It may seem like these people are detached from their feelings and incapable of showing emotion; however, this is not true. We are all human, and we all experience the same types of emotions. The difference is that they are keeping theirs locked up.

Not only are they keeping their emotions hidden from the outside world, they are most often, hiding their feelings from themselves as well. They try to put it out of their consciousness and bury their problems deep down inside. These feelings and emotions try escaping and rear their heads from time to time, which creates a lot of internal conflict and suffering. They have little regard for their own feelings; therefore, it is nearly impossible for them to be sensitive towards other people's feelings. Although they may want to, they are incapable of physically or verbally showing compassion. They become uncomfortable when other people express their feelings, and this comes across as rude and insensitive.

I think this is a contributing factor to many failed relationships. If one of the parties involved is not being honest about their feelings, a couple's communication breaks down. If one person is not expressing their true self and instead is acting out in an irrational manner, this causes major problems and unresolvable conflicts. If the trapped energy gets to its boiling point, one can lose control all together. It can become dangerous, and it can unintentionally come out aggressively and even violently.

Trapped Energy can also be perceived as cold and egotistical; the term 'ice princess' comes to mind. People who do not show a lot of emotion can come across as non-engaging, detached, and self-centered. Because they are uncomfortable with their own feelings, non-emotional people can be a little standoffish. A person who wears his or her heart on their sleeve is often generalized as warm and loving, and a person who keeps their feelings hidden can be considered aloof and unfriendly.

Although it may not be true, the perception is that these people are high on themselves, and/or that they think they are better than others. As a result, they do not make friends easily, and it is difficult for them to be in deep meaningful relationships. Because they do not let people in, others find it difficult to truly get to know them.

Lastly, at the other end of the spectrum, *Trapped Energy* people can be seen as amazing, kind, positive people who have no problems of their own. They constantly hear things like, "you never get emotional and are always so calm, collected, and positive," and, "you're lucky because you don't have any problems or worries," and, "your life is so perfect." People hold these types of people to high standards, look up to them, and put them on a pedestal of sorts.

Others create high expectations for these people, and this energy type feels like he or she has to live up to them at all cost. When they do get upset or emotional, they often feel guilty about it and keep it to themselves. They are afraid to change people's perceptions of them, and/or do not want to burden others with their problems. As a result, they may be carrying a fake persona. This makes them feel lonely, isolated, and conflicted. When you are faking your emotions, the only person you are fooling is yourself.

Ultimately it doesn't really matter how people perceive a *Trapped Energy* person. They are all equally dangerous. Of all the energy types, this one has the most severe consequences and devastating effects on people's lives. Again, all humans create both positive and negative energy inside of their bodies. Expressing feelings and emotions, talking to others, and acting upon emotions are some of the ways energy is released.

This energy is released from the inside out—through the skin and eventually out into the universe. Although emitting negative energy impacts your human energy field, sticks to your aura, and impacts your life, it is still vital that you release it. Once released, the negative energy can be combated and destroyed by the positive energy you create, and by the positive energy that already exists in the universe. Remember a small amount of positive energy can destroy mountains of negative energy. It is stronger, and a lot more powerful.

A Trapped Energy type of person literally has trapped negative energy, which is entombed inside of his or her body. Energy is not static; it is in constant motion. In this case, the kinetic energy has nowhere to go, so it keeps moving around and vibrating inside the body. Eventually the energy becomes stale, potent, and toxic. This can become extremely dangerous!

Positive energy is commonly described as healthy energy, and negative energy is called unhealthy energy. For me the obvious association is that unhealthy negative energy can literally make a person unhealthy. I believe that trapped energy has the potential to make a person physically ill. Negative energy sticks to your cells, your bones, and your organs. It can turn into headaches, physical ailments, and even into diseases.

Perhaps this is why medical problems and diseases are most common in older people. Years and years of pent up negative energy eventually over-takes the body and creates a series of health problems. They have created lifelong habits, which do not allow them to release their negative energy in an effective and efficient manner. Seniors are less likely to change their energy type. Also, the older people get, the less interested others are in hearing their problems, so sadly they are forced, by society, to keep their feelings and emotions trapped inside.

In our generation, people are getting sicker at a much younger age than before. Medical and scientific advancements should be eliminating ill-nesses, yet life-threatening diseases are on the rise. Health problems once known only to senior citizens are now occurring in young adults. People are having heart attacks in their 30s and 40s, depression and suicides happen to people of all ages, and health care around the world is in a serious state of calamity. I think that Trapped Energy is a contributing factor in many of these cases.

Slowly but surely you need to find a way to release this pent up energy. You simply need to stop being a person who is a Trapped Energy type. Crying is a great way of physically releasing pent up energy. After a good cry people often feel relaxed, less anxious, and physically lighter.

I know this woman, who is often considered insensitive and aloof by her family and friends. She is clearly a Trapped Energy type of person and difficult to get to know. Through countless conversations, I eventually got her to break down her barriers. She admitted that, although she is not a very emotional person, she does feel things on the inside. She told me that she often breaks down and cries alone in the shower. However, she fights hard against her emotions, and she tells herself to, *suck it up*, and, *get over it*, and to, *quit being a baby*. I have since conversed with many people who speak to themselves in a similar manner.

If you can relate to this, and if you see yourself as a Trapped Energy person, I hope you understand that these are harsh words to say to others, and even harsher words to tell yourself. It should make you wonder how you learned to treat yourself this way. If you think about it, you may agree that these statements, and this type of sentiment, came from other people in your life. Perhaps while growing up your parents or siblings said things like this to you. Maybe a spouse or significant other responded to your emotions in this punitive manner.

Over time, you internalized this irrational response to normal natural human feelings, and you turned it into expectations for yourself. I have said it many times, you have to have compassion for your feelings, and you have to stop being so hard on yourself. It is time to break these self-deprecating thought patterns and allow yourself to feel. After all, if you are not feeling, you are not truly living. Feelings and emotions are what make us human. When they are guided by our soul, they represent the essence of who we are. They should never be looked down upon or ignored. I will say it again, if you are not feeling, you are not truly living.

If crying is not your thing, then get yourself alone in a room and yell, scream, or throw things—just make sure you do so in a safe and responsible manner. Run, exercise, or take boxing lessons. Do whatever you can to physically release some of the pent up energy. Remember actions release stronger amounts of energy then thoughts, feelings, and emotions.

You can start by releasing your stale negative energy all alone, but eventually you will have to learn how to do so by communicating with others. You need to be able to verbalize how you are feeling. You have to be able to discuss your feelings with your loved ones. You may have to swallow your pride and become vulnerable. You may have to force yourself to be uncomfortable at first. By being uncomfortable in the beginning, you will gain comfort like you have never experienced before.

The first step is to identify that you are a Trapped Energy type and admit it to yourself. The second step is to admit it to your family and friends. As hard as it may be, you have to communicate this problem with the people in your life and ask for their patience, their understanding, and their assistance. It is okay to say things like, "I realize that I am the type of person who keeps things bottled up inside, and I don't properly express my feeling or emotions, and I want to change that about myself," or, "on the inside I am very sensitive, I just don't know how to show that side of myself to you," or, "I need some help expressing all of the negative emotions I have pent up inside in a rational way, and I want your help."

Some of you may be reading this rolling your eyes. You may be thinking that this will make you sound silly and it isn't your style, but then I ask: what is the alternative to not doing so? Divorce, being disconnected from your parents or children, having no friends or getting physical ailments and diseases are realistic outcomes. If you do not stop being a Trapped Energy person every aspect of your life will eventually be impacted.

You may be thinking that you are the only person with this problem and that people will not understand you, but you will be surprised how many people out there are suffering the same way you are. I assure you the people in your life will be relieved, thankful, and eager to help. They will finally understand you. In this manner, you will truly let people into your internal world. You will create much deeper and more meaningful relationships and live a healthier happier life.

Make it a dinner table ritual to talk about the highs and lows you each experienced during the day. US President Barack Obama and his family use 'the rose and the thorn' analogy to get their family to discuss their feelings. The rose symbolizes the good thing that happened that day, and the thorn is something that happened that wasn't so great. According to my theory, the thorn represents something that may have created some negative energy inside of you.

If every person in our world found safe, effective, and efficient ways of releasing their negative energy, I think that the divorce rate would go down, families would stay connected, life expectancy would increase, and violence and crime would decrease. We would be a much calmer, more rational, and civil global society.

Before proceeding answer the following questions:

1. What energy type are you currently?

2. Have you always been this energy type or has it changed in the past?

3. I want you to think about your life thus far as a timeline. In the squares boxes below write down monumental events that have happened in your life. Some examples are childhood, high school graduation, started dating a boyfriend/girlfriend, marriage, the death of a loved one, an injury or illness, childbirth, a significant vacation, divorce etc. Then on the top line I want you to identify what your energy was like during that phase. On the bottom line I want you to write down if you were primarily creating positive energy during that time or negative energy during that time.

4. Reflect back. What does your changing energy types say about your life?

5. How has your energy impacted your life?

6. Going forward, what steps will you take to manage and protect your energy?

CHAPTER 17: EnLIGHTenment

White light often represents purity and divinity. Countless people, who have had near death experiences, have come back to life and explained how they were drawn towards a white light. Many religions also use white light symbolically in reference to the divine creator.

In spiritual terms, white light embodies the divine source of love. This is basically what God is—a divine source of pure love that knows no boundaries, has no limits, and has no flaws. It is the strongest force that exists in the physical and non-physical realities.

I strongly believe that we are all born with the white light of God within us. As babies we are completely filled with this divine light from head to toe. It is like a candle burning bright and strong. This light guides us and protects us. Like a giant umbilical cord, it connects us to God and to all that God has created. Over time as our mind becomes more active and dominant, we get attached to worldly things, and we detach from our soul, the light starts to slowly diminish inside of us. The light dims faster in some people than in others based on upbringing, circumstances, and how people choose to exercise their free will.

Because this light exists within every single living being, we are all born pure; we are all born righteous, and we are all born out of divine love. There is some innate good in everyone, even those people who choose to do harmful and immoral things. Being dishonest, corrupt, and cruel to other living beings in the world affects the amount of white light you carry inside. Unfortunately these people only carry a small flicker of God's light within them. They manage to destroy and disconnect from the divine guidance, and this is why they are capable of being cold and heartless; however, a glimmer of the light still remains to exist within them deep down inside.

It is important for us to enlighten ourselves, and to bring back as much of God's light as we can. This light will empower us, protect us, and connect us with the creator. Also it is vital for us as parents, and as a society, to ensure that the bright light that exists within children does not start to diminish.

Now that we understand how energy and what I call the energy equilibrium works, we cannot deny that negative people and negative energy exists all around us. It is impossible for us to avoid it because it is an important and realistic part of life. Again, there is a reason why we are in this world with billions of other people. God could have easily put us on individual islands, where we could sit in meditation and prayer all day long, but God chose not to for very specific reasons.

We are constantly interacting and learning from the people around us. Fortunately—and unfortunately—this impacts our lives, and our energy, both positively and negatively. Although we share our lives with billions of other people, God loves us individually and has created tools that we can use to protect ourselves and our loved ones.

If someone tries to attack you with a fist, a knife, or a gun you would protect yourself with your arms, a shield, or by using a similar weapon. In the same manner, if someone attacks your aura by draining you of your positive energy, or leaves their negative energy in your human energy field, then you need to take action to protect yourself also; this is where the concept of wrapping yourself in white light comes in.

I have heard numerous people in interviews and on television say that they wrap themselves in white light all the time—including Oprah Winfrey. However, what does this mean exactly? No it does not mean that you take a string of white light bulbs and wrap yourself it in like a Christmas tree. It is more of a visualization that manifests as a non-visual reality. You cannot see it, but it does exist.

Light varies in wavelengths, and therefore, it is a form of energy. This energy resonates and affects all living things. As we absorb light energy from the universe, it passes through our human energy field and sticks to our aura. It then passes through our eyes and skin and affects the energy we carry within. It has even been scientifically proven that light is stored in our DNA.

Before the invention of herbal remedies and medications, people used to heal themselves and each other by using light energy. Different colors of light have different wavelengths, which means they are different types of energy. Each color of light has its own purpose and power: some are healers, some are protectors, and others provide spiritual guidance. Today Color Therapy and other forms of energy healing techniques— including Reiki—are used as non-medicinal healing methods.

Because the color white is identified as the pure light of God, we can invoke the divine presence within us and protect ourselves by using it. By connecting with the white light you are connecting with the deep rich source of all life and love. The white light creates an armor, which is always available to you on command. At any given moment, you can put on this armor and use it. It protects you against bad thoughts, negative energy, fear, worry, or anything that can hurt or harm you.

There are several ways you can wrap yourself in white light. I did some research and read different people's theories on how this process should be done. I was thinking I would provide you with insight on what has been written on this subject, and allow you to choose the method that works best for you. Some say that you have to create shapes with the light, others say you have to wrap yourself in the light a certain number of times, and some experts specify what body position you need to be in before you bring in light. However, none of these methods resonated as being 100% true to me. I am not saying that they are incorrect, I am sure they are all equally effective, but I feel they are unnecessary.

I have already explained, in great detail, that our intentions are one of the most powerful tools that we have. God, our spirit guides, and the angels can read our intent, and they will act upon our wishes. Therefore, I think that in order for you to wrap yourself in white light, all you have to do is intend it to be so. All you need to do is visualize it and call it, and it will be there.

You can do this in whichever way feels most comfortable for you. It doesn't matter if you do it sitting, standing, or lying down. It doesn't matter if you are in deep meditation, in the shower, or stuck in traffic. You can say it out loud verbally or write it on your chalkboard in the sky. This will all ultimately accomplish the same thing. Personally, I think that rules and guidelines simply interfere in spiritual processes, and unnecessarily complicate things. The less rules and techniques you attach to it, the easier it will be for you to connect to the light. Again, there is no wrong way of doing it.

Simply ask your spirit guides and angels to bring the white light into your mind, into your body, into your soul, and into your understanding. Ask to be surrounded by white light, and imagine it all around you and within you. It is as easy as that. I personally imagine that I am sitting inside of a giant egg, or inside of a giant round crystal. I feel the white light coming through the top of the egg or crystal.

If I am going into an environment where I know that a lot of tension and negative energy exists—for instance if people are gossiping in front of me or if someone is constantly complaining, being pessimistic, and creating unnecessary drama around me—then I take one extra precaution. I start by wrapping myself in white light. I then expand the white light out and around myself as far as I can possibly envision it to be; I create a gigantic bubble of white light around myself. Then, through visualization, I place mirrors all along the outside of my bubble.

This way, because of the mirrored border, negative energy will reflect and redirect back to where it came from. It will bounce off of me and directly go back on to the person who sent it. I have noticed that certain people, who are mean-spirited and constantly talk bad about others, have stopped doing so around me. Due to the energy equilibrium, they are subconsciously trying to give me their negative energy and take my positive energy. In the past, talking to me has made them feel better, but since I have been protecting myself in this manner, it doesn't work anymore.

Because of the mirrored shield around me, their negative energy simply reflects off of me and sticks back onto them. They likely don't feel very good afterwards. Eventually they are subconsciously forced to stop being negative and creating unnecessary drama around me. Hopefully these people will then learn to stop creating so much negative energy. Instead of taking your positive energy, they will be responsible for creating positive energy of their own. The mirrored shield can also help protect you against people who are jealous or envious of you—and from anyone who may be wishing ill upon you.

You can also extend white light, and your armor, out to your friends, relatives, and loved ones. Bring the white light into your own sphere and then send it out to others. See the light creating a wall of protection, or a mirrored bubble of white light around them. When you send people white light, you are basically sending them love. Love that will manifest as positive energy—which will stick to their surroundings, to their auras, and seep through their skin—to help heal and protect them from the inside out.

CHAPTER 18: VIBRATIONS

It is scientific fact that all things have a vibration. Every molecule in our body has a specific vibration, and every molecule in the universe has a specific vibration. Every living being vibrates at its own frequency: some vibrational frequencies are similar to each other, and some things vibrate at completely different levels. It is through vibrations and frequencies that everything is in constant communication.

A great deal of scientific research has been done on energy and vibrations. It is simple physics. I want to discuss the important part that vibrations play in relation to spirituality. The frequency at which we vibrate affects our day-to-day lives, our souls, the universe and the spirit world.

Take a look at the pyramid of hierarchy that I discussed in Chapter 7.

I had identified that God resides at the top of the pyramid, in the highest realm possible—in a divine and pure form, which is indescribable and unexplainable. Directly below God's realm is the spirit world, and below this is the universe in which planet earth exists. I also mentioned in Chapter 8 that I believe a realm exists below our physical world, and I will get to that in the next chapter.

I have spent a lot of time in meditation and in deep thought trying to understand how these different realms are connected, how they differ, and how they communicate. The answer I received is that vibrations hold an important key to understanding our physical and non-physical realities. I believe that you can only see and experience things that vibrate on a similar frequency as you. The different vibrations can be described as either high and low or fast and slow; it means the same thing.

Without a shadow of a doubt God vibrates at the highest or fastest level possible. The creator resides alone in a divine frequency that is immeasurable and unattainable. This is why it is impossible for anyone to fully understand, define, or see God. It is simply at a whole other vibrational frequency.

The spirit world also vibrates at an incredibly high level or fast speed. Within the spirit world there are also different degrees of vibrational frequencies. Archangels, to recap, are extremely powerful. They can subdivide into five or six billion and help everyone if they are called upon— they are as close to God as anything can be. If they are the strongest spirits in the spirit world, then it is natural to assume that they vibrate at the highest frequency possible in the spirit world. Directly below the archangels, is the frequency at which our spirit guides vibrate. Underneath them are the angels, and beneath the angels are the spirits of all the beings that have passed away and reside in the spirit world.

There is a logical chain of command that exists in the spirit world; however, all of them vibrate at a much higher level or faster speed than any human being has the potential of reaching. This makes a lot of sense. Humans do not vibrate on the same frequency as the spirit world, and as a result, we are unable to fully understand them, unable to see them, and unable to experience them in the manner in which they exist.

As I mentioned before, when a spirit takes on a life as a living organism, it shifts form from a spirit into a soul. Souls vibrate at many different levels, which are available within a certain spectrum or scale. This spectrum or scale is predetermined—or preset—only for living organisms that exist within our universe. Each realm has its own set of frequencies. The vibrational frequencies available in our universe are completely different then the vibrational frequencies available in the spirit world. Again you can only see and experience things that vibrate on a similar frequency as you. I believe that God intentionally did this so humans can be submerged in their present reality.

A person's vibrational frequency correlates to the amount of divine white light they carry inside. God and God's white light protects us and keeps us connected with the divine creator. Our spirit guides and angels communicate with us and guide us. They inadvertently help us vibrate at a higher level. Babies are filled with white light from head to toe. They vibrate at the highest possible frequency that exists within the universe. Disconnecting from one's soul, pessimistic intentions, and negative energy all lower our vibrational level. People who only have a flicker of white light in them vibrate at an incredible low level.

Here on earth, people who vibrate at similar levels, communicate on similar frequencies. Without physically meeting or interacting, our vibrations have the potential of communicating with others. I think this is yet another way the Law of Attraction works: like attracts like. People who are on similar frequencies will eventually meet one another, and form bonds and relationships. They communicate on a whole other, nonverbal level.

This can be a good thing and a bad thing. On the plus side, if you are a positive person who is vibrating on a high frequency, the universe will connect you with other people who are like you. These people will be drawn to your life by a force that supersedes your efforts. Eventually you will get together and share your positive outlook on life. You will better one another's lives, experience, and consequently raise one another's vibrational levels even higher.

Since I have started on my spiritual journey, I cannot begin to tell you how many people I have met who are on a similar path. Everywhere I go, I meet spiritual people who are positive and have incredible stories.

Unintentionally the conversation always leads to subjects pertaining to spirituality. It is blatantly obvious to me that people were sent my way in order to help me with this book.

However, the vibrational Law of Attraction is not always helpful in one's life. On the downside, if you are a pessimistic person—who is on a downward spiral in your life—you are likely to meet others who are equally lost and suffering. The Law of Attraction works both ways; regardless of the type of person you are, it will attract people who are like you and bring them into your life. What you are like is a consequence of your free will; remember God and God's helpers cannot interfere in your free will.

Drug addicts and alcoholics meet other drug addicts and alcoholics, high school drop outs run into others who have left school, and depressed people are drawn towards other depressed people. These people all have similar sentiments and outlooks on life, so they end up dragging each other down. Eventually they further decrease each other's vibrational frequency.

If you increase your vibrational frequency, you will communicate with other positive people who also vibrate at a higher or faster frequency. You will be aligned with these people and they will be drawn to your life. These people will likely bring you happiness, and help you find meaning and purpose in your life. Increasing your vibrational frequency will also protect you and keep negative and pessimistic people away from you.

Everything that exists has a vibrational frequency. Furthermore, I think that each vibrational frequency has to stay within certain parameters. There is a certain scale to which everything is confined. There are limitations on how high you can vibrate, and there is a certain vibrational threshold that you cannot drop below. In other words, you can only rise so high up and you are only capable of sinking so far down.

God and God's helpers have a much larger range in which they can vibrate at. Their vibrational frequency spectrum is a lot more flexible than the one available to humans. Spirit guides and angels are constantly interacting with humans on earth. They have to decrease their vibrational level in order to communicate with us and guide us. However, they can only come so far down. Also they can only vibrate at a lower frequency for a certain amount of time. They then have to go back up and recharge before they can come back down again.

There is a certain predetermined vibrational threshold that your spirit guides and angels are not capable of crossing. They simply cannot vibrate below that line. There is no frequency available to them down there. If you are vibrating below that threshold, then your spirit guides and angels have no choice but to hover above and watch you go down the wrong path. They are unable to guide you, and they are unable to protect you.

If life kicks your butt, so to speak, and you are consumed with negative energy, this consequently decreases your vibrational level. Other internal and external factors—such as disconnecting from your soul, not knowing who you are, allowing your mind to take control, and/or using your free will to hurt or harm other living beings—may lead you to further lower your vibrational frequency. Throughout your life, if your vibrational level keeps dropping, eventually a point may come when your spirit guides and angels are no longer able to reach you. No matter how badly the spirit world may want to help you, they cannot. Again they take your vibrational frequency as an indication of your free will. You have made choices and decisions that lead you to vibrate at that low frequency, and they cannot interfere in your free will.

When this happens people get into serious trouble. They make wrong decisions, lose their purpose in life, and have a difficult time getting back on the right path. They have the potential to become seriously depressed, suicidal, and/or morally corrupt. In this state, people often try to escape the confusion and the suffering by numbing their brains. They may try to avoid their problems by turning to sex, gambling, drugs, or alcohol.

Drugs and alcohol make matters worse. Intoxication reduces your vibrational frequency. If you are already vibrating at a low level, then drugs and alcohol are a poison for your soul. Perhaps this is why most religions tell people to stay away from them. Being in an intoxicated state gives you a false sense of security. It drains your energy, and it attacks your vibrational frequency and lowers it.

This is why it is so vital to keep your vibrational level as high as possible. The higher you vibrate, the more protected and guided you are. You will have a strong sense of intuition that will help you make right decisions, and you will understand and follow your purpose in life. Overall you will be wiser, healthier, and happier.

Sitting in a bath is not only relaxing, but I have heard that it also increases your vibrational level. A Reiki master once told me that being submerged in water, and simultaneously being grounded by your bath tub, can increase your vibrations by three times. The bathtub is a great place to write on your chalkboard in the sky and to communicate with your spirit guides and angels. I have been doing this for the past year or so, and I find the most spiritual clarity and internal calmness when I am in the bath.

I hope that it is now becoming clear that everything in this book is directly interrelated; this is because everything in our physical and non-physical realities is similarly interrelated. Connecting with your soul, proactively communicating with your spirit guides, creating positive energy, and bringing in white light simultaneously increases your vibrational frequency.

If you fail to do spiritual work, and your vibrational frequency keeps dropping, then you open yourself up to one more very serious problem. The most dangerous consequence of being on a very low vibrational frequency is that you become visible to the 4th realm in the pyramid. This is the realm that exists beneath the universe and our physical world. You have the potential to vibrate on a similar frequency as entities that exist in the paranormal world.

Ideas. Thought. Questions

_____

_____

CHAPTER 19: PARANORMAL WORLD

As I have discussed before, I believe that there are four different realms in our reality. Each realm exists independently; however, they are all connected. To recap my pyramid of hierarchy, God's realm is at the top of the hierarchy. Below God's realm is the spirit world, and below that is the universe in which we live. Again each realm vibrates at different frequencies. One can only see or experience things that vibrate on his or her individual frequency. Humans do not typically vibrate high enough, or fast enough, to see and experience the realms that exist above the physical world. They also do not typically vibrate low enough, or slow enough, to see and experience the realm that exists below the universe. However, this is not always the case.

The time has now come to discuss the 4th and final realm, which can be described as the paranormal world. This realm is perhaps the most misunderstood. This is an unknown world tainted by thousands of years of myth, speculation, and fear. There is something within human nature that enjoys being frightened and startled. Haunted houses, ghost stories, and horror films intrigue us as a society. From urban legends, to campfire stories, to novels, to films, an entire horror genre has been created. This phenomenon has impacted humans so much so that a special day has been created in its honor—Halloween—and is celebrated annually in many countries around the world.

The paranormal world is typically associated with ghosts, goblins, and negative entities. Some religions believe that it is a world run by the devil, who is an evil, immoral, and completely dissipated entity. The devil is considered God's enemy who created his own world to spite God: a world called hell. I have spent a lot of time contemplating and thinking about the notion of hell.

None of my soul searching and meditation has led me to believe in a hell. God's love is far too great, and far too powerful, for such a place to exist. In *Conversations with God: an uncommon dialogue*, Neale Donald Walsch asks God what is hell? According to Walsch God answered, "hell does not exist as this place you have fantasized, where you burn in some everlasting fire, or exist in some state of everlasting torment. What purpose could I have in that? Even if I did hold the extraordinarily ungodly thought that you did not "deserve" heaven, why would I have a need to seek some kind of revenge, or punishment, for your failing?"

There are good life lessons to be learned about temptation, immorality, and consequences from the concept of hell; however, I believe it was all meant metaphorically. Somewhere along historic lines, it was interpreted literally.

I also do not believe that everything in the paranormal world is negative, scary, or dangerous. Our perception of ghosts, goblins, and evil entities is not an accurate depiction. It is a stereotype that comes from figments of people's imagination. They are also driven by people's fear.

I think that the ego develops fear from not knowing and/or not understanding something. If you do not know something, and you are incapable of understanding it, then naturally you feel like you cannot control it; being out of control leads to baseless thoughts and emotions that create fear.

I personally spent a year absolutely inundated by fear-driven thoughts about the paranormal world. I don't know what set it off. I was always afraid of scary stories and horror films, but I got to a point where I was completely consumed by this realm. My imagination created frightening images of ghosts and scary beings. I constantly felt afraid and anxious. I was paranoid that something was around me, and I frequently suffered with nightmares. I was even scared to go out at night sometimes. I should point out that this occurred around the same time my faith wavered, and I doubted the existence of a God. I was depressed and probably vibrating at a lower level.

Anyhow, I understand how paralyzing and dangerous fear truly can be. For me, the only way I could stop being afraid was to face it head on. I started listening to people's scary stories and talking about the subject more often. One day I forced myself to go and watch the movie *The Exorcism of Emily Rose*, which is based on a true story about a girl who is possessed and then goes through an exorcism. Surprisingly, I found the advertisements for the film to be much more frightening than the actual movie.

Over time I started to feel better, and the fear stopped consuming me. However, it wasn't until I went through my spiritual journey and connected with my soul, that I actually became completely fearless about this subject. I do not want anyone to be afraid of anything. This is why I am trying to explain all the unknown realities that affect our human experience. The paranormal world is definitely one of those unknowns.

I know that many people would rather just avoid this subject altogether. You may be afraid to read about it. However, this chapter is not meant to scare you. Talking about this and exploring it head on will take away the power it has to frighten you. You will realize that it wasn't anything scary after all. If talking about angels, spirit guides, and the spirit world hasn't scared you, then this chapter shouldn't either. However, if you wish to skip this chapter, go ahead and proceed to chapter 20 now.

So what is the paranormal world? Who resides there, and why? First off, the single most important thing we need to remember is that God created every single thing that is in existence. Everything has been created through God's divine love. As I have already discussed, in the beginning God existed alone in his or her own divine realm. God then created the spirit world and countless individual spirits. Spirit guides, angels, humans and all other beings began their journey as spirits who lived in the spirit world. Therefore anything that exists in the paranormal world also started off as a spirit that came from God, a spirit that was divinely created out of love, light, and goodness.

As we have discussed, when a spirit enters a living organism — takes birth here on the planet Earth—it shifts form, lowers its vibrational frequency, and transitions into what we call a soul. When a person dies his or her soul increases its vibrational frequency and crosses-over back into spirit form. The spirit then returns to exist in the spirit world. However, this is not always the case.

Sometimes, due to various reasons, a soul does not go back into its original spirit form. Instead, at the time of death, a person's vibrational frequency drops, and its energy transitions into a form, which we can call an entity. Simultaneously, the entity leaves the universe—and the realm of the physical world—and begins to exist in the 4th realm, which is the paranormal world.

I am calling this realm the paranormal world, but just like the spirit world, the word *world* is simply a metaphor. There is no physical world or planet there. Its existence is indescribable and unexplainable because humans do not vibrate at that low frequency. Because we do not vibrate at that frequency, we are unable to see it and experience it in its true form. It is outside the scope of our understanding.

As I have already explained, God has created specific parameters and thresholds that everything must vibrate within. We can only go so far up the vibrational frequency levels, and we can only come so far down. Spirit guides and angels can only decrease their vibrational frequency level a certain amount in order to guide us, protect us, and communicate with us. This is why it is so important for humans to constantly keep their energy and vibrations high. If we start to vibrate below the threshold at which angels can vibrate, then we are no longer guided and protected. Spirit guides and angels have no choice but to hover above and watch us make wrong choices and go down an unguided path. Again, our vibrational level is an indication of our free will, and God and God's helpers cannot interfere in one's free will.

Entities existing in the paranormal world vibrate at an incredibly low frequency. They are well below the threshold at which spirit guides and angels are capable of vibrating. Unless they somehow increase their vibrational level, spirit guides and angels are unable to contact them, communicate with them, and or guide them. They have no choice but to watch entities fall off the radar, so to speak.

This is where it gets a little complicated. Remember, our human experience, our physical world, and the universe all exist in a realm, which is defined by time and space. When any living being dies, it is no longer living in a realm defined by time and space. Because entities exist outside the realm of time and space, time is not a factor for them. They can spend hundreds and even thousands of human years in the paranormal world.

Humans are impacted by the paranormal world because sometimes our worlds collide. Sometimes entities try to reenter our world and use our space. They do so because they are trying to find a way to increase their vibrational level. Entities need to get on a higher vibrational frequency in order to crossover into spirit form. Humans are the next level up. It's like climbing up a ladder. Entities need to go up the vibrational frequency ladder from the paranormal world, through the physical world, and then eventually up to the spirit world. This is why so many humans have had contact with entities. This is why people have experienced the paranormal world to some extent.

These beings are often called negative entities. Their energy may be negatively charged, but they are not necessarily negative, evil, or scary. Many of them do not even realize that they are dead and no longer in human form. Sometimes when people die a very sudden and shocking death, and they are vibrating at a low frequency at the time of their death—which cannot be reached by their spirit guides and angels—they lack the guidance and support they require to crossover back into spirit form. As a consequence they can be oblivious to their death. Although their energy has changed form and transitioned from a soul into an entity, in their mind, they are still living their human life as usual.

I believe that they create an alternative reality that looks exactly like their human life. They live in their homes, drive in their cars, and go places, even though none of their physical things exist anymore. Even if their house burns down, and a hundred years later a new house gets built in its place, in their reality their original house is still there. When new tenants move into the house, the entities are confused and think that the people are intruding on their space.

The two realities then become blurred and disoriented to them. The entities are not necessarily evil or dangerous. They are simply bothered by the noise humans make. They may do things to try and get people to leave their space. Humans interpret this as a haunted or possessed house. This has been the plot of hundreds of horror films over the years.

In other circumstances, some entities are aware that their bodies have died, and that they are no longer in human form. However, they are lost, confused, and unable to crossover due to their low vibrational level. They do not understand their transition. They go from place to place trying to figure out what happened and what caused their death—sometimes these entities may look to humans for help.

In other cases, some soul's may purposely choose not to crossover. As portrayed in the movie *Sixth Sense*, written and directed by M. Night Shyamalan, some souls become entities because they have unfinished business here on earth. They are not ready to go into the white light and transfer their energy back into a spirit. They choose to stay back to try and help and protect their loved ones and/or to get revenge for their death. Again, because they are vibrating at a low level, they are unable to seek proper guidance from the spirit world. People can crossover into spirit form and still look after and protect their loved ones who are still here on Earth, although there is far too much love and understanding in the spirit world for the concept of revenge to exist.

The only types of entities we have to worry about are the same type of humans we have to worry about here on earth. Sadly there are many humans who use their free will to harm, deceive, and torment others. Through their thoughts and actions they create negative energy, and they push God's divine light out of their bodies. As a result they too vibrate at a lower frequency than most others.

At the time of their death, they may be afraid of their own preconceived notions about judgment or God's wrath. They try to avoid the consequences that they feel they may face in the spirit world. Their souls choose not to go into the light and crossover back into spirit. In the paranormal world they follow the same path they walked in the physical world. As entities they continue to be callous, corrupt, and dangerous.

So what do we do to protect ourselves? The most important thing we should do is to keep our vibrational levels high and keep as much of God's light and love within ourselves as possible. If you are vibrating at a relatively high frequency, no one in the paranormal world can even see you. You are unreachable to them. You walk into any space and automatically clear the energy. Entities are incapable of being anywhere near your human energy field. You will likely never have an encounter, or experience a situation that involves them; therefore, you do not need to fear them. You never have to think about the paranormal world.

If you are connected to your soul, then let your intuition guide you. If your gut tells you that something is not quite right—that it may be related to something from the paranormal world— then take that seriously and do something about it. Just like spirit guides and angels, entities can also hear and understand your intent. If you feel a presence in your home or around you, you can simply tell it to go away. Get strong with your words and command it to leave your space and your world.

I personally do not think that you need to call in any psychics or experts to deal with entities. Each one of us is stronger and much more powerful than we know. Make your intent known and the entities will follow your orders and leave. You can also call upon your spirit guides and angels to help you. They will provide you with all the backup, support, and protection you need.

The only external thing that I would suggest is getting some sage. Sage is a natural herb that is believed to neutralize energy. Just open the doors and windows in your home or work space and burn some sage in all your rooms. This will get rid of any stale unhealthy energy that the entity may have left behind.

Because entities are not necessarily negative or evil, I think that humans should try to have some compassion and empathy for them; they may be lost, confused, or simply looking for guidance. Believe it or not, if you choose to, you are powerful enough to help them crossover back to the spirit world. You can do what spirit guides and angels are unable to do because of their vibrational restrictions. You can serve as a medium between the paranormal world and the spirit world. Through visualization and intention, you can show them the way.

Before you show compassion for an entity and try to help it, you must first protect yourself. You do not know exactly what you are dealing with, so do not take any chances. Here are some suggested tips to follow:

1. First and foremost, call upon your spirit guides and angels to help you with this situation. Write it on your chalkboard in the sky and assign a task.

2. Second, wrap yourself in white light and extend that white light out to your family, friends, and to your surroundings. No entity can permeate the white light of God. Most of them will leave as soon as you do this.

3. The third step is to get strong with your words and tell the entity to leave.

4. Then you can say a prayer and ask it to follow the white light and crossover into spirit form. Through prayer, visualization, and intent you can reassure the entity that God is forgiving and loving, and in the spirit world it will get all the guidance and support it needs.

5. Lastly, remove any stale, dark, or unhealthy energy that the entity may have left behind in your aura and/or in your surroundings. Open some windows, burn some sage in the affected surroundings, and/or ask the angels to neutralize the energy for you.

6.   Finally, relax, feel safe, and be confident that the entity has left. Don't give it another thought. Continue to wrap yourself and your loved ones in white light and keep increasing your vibrational frequency. Reassure yourself that it was nothing frightening or scary. It was just some lost energy that was passing by. It has found its way home now, and it won't bother you anymore.

There is one last thing that I want to talk about in regards to the paranormal world, and that is children's abilities to see and experience entities. I think that children, because they are still filled with so much of God's white light, have a larger range at which they can vibrate at. They can vibrate at an incredibly high frequency and experience seeing angels. They may also be able to see the spirits of deceased family members who live in the spirit world. Similarly they can also vibrate on a much lower frequency than adults.

Entities can sense when children have this ability, and that is why they sometimes reach out to them for help and guidance. This obviously confuses children and can scare them. If a child in your life expresses to you that they have experienced seeing someone or something that you cannot see, don't dismiss it right away. Connect with your own soul and ask your spirit guides and angels to tell you if this is a figment of the child's imagination or an actual fact.

Wrap your child in white light every day, and teach your child how to wrap him or herself in the white light; again, entities cannot permeate the protection created by the white light. Also follow the steps outlined above to make the entity go away. Even if you are not sure, it doesn't hurt to clean the energy in your surroundings every once in a while.

Ideas. Thoughts. Questions.

_____

_____

_____

CHAPTER 20: WHY ARE WE HERE?

Now that we have identified and defined the realms that exist around us, let's come back and focus on our realm and our reality. Why are we here? I used to think that God created Earth as a place of worship—a place souls came to pray, meditate, and live in God's glory—but look around; Earth is definitely not solely a place of worship. From what we know about our history, it never has been. All living organisms have survival instincts, free will, and a mind that is independent from the body and the soul. If the Earth was intended solely as a place of worship, why do all these other factors exist?

I have already established that Earth is not a place where God sends souls to be judged and tested. God loves us, and it is within God's will to give humans free will. God would never give humans free will and then judge and scrutinize every choice and decision which is made. All the material goods, relationships, and temptations that exist in our physical world are not attractions or distractions that lead us down the right or wrong path. Again, it is mankind that categorizes things as right or wrong—as good or bad. There is no such distinction according to God and the spirit world.

So then why? Why did God create our universe, and why do spirits change their energy into souls in order to live life? Why do humans experience relationships, struggles, hunger, pain, love, success and so many other things? The answer is right in front of us. If you think about it, every single thing that happens in our lives—every high and every low—teaches us something. They serve as lessons that help us develop and grow. These lessons are what we come to earth for.

Everything in God's realm and in the spirit world is perfect, innocent, and pure. There is no anger, no fighting, no loss, no grieving and no suffering; too much love and understanding exists there for any of this to ever develop. There are no problems or adversities in the spirit world from which spirits can learn and grow. It is a place where worldly issues do not matter.

Just like a fetus sitting comfortably in a mother's womb, spirits are surrounded by love and protection. As parents, we bring children into this world so we can love them and nurture them. We want to protect them and be with them all the time; however, we do many things to ensure that our children learn, grow, and develop. We take them on trips and vacations to experience different cultures, to see what Mother Nature has to offer, and to create memories. We eventually let go of our children and send them off to college, where they gain so much more than just an education. They learn about socializing, relationships, structure, academics and about having fun. They develop so many different skills, which come in handy later on in their lives.

Although parents don't want their children to be harmed or to have their hearts broken, they know that every time they get hurt they learn and they grow. They learn more from their mistakes then they do from their accomplishments. Parents want all of these opportunities for their children, and Gods wants the same things for us all.

My spiritual journey has led me to the following conclusion: in the very beginning God existed alone in His or Her own glory. No one knows how God came into existence, when, or why. We have to accept this as a reality that we are incapable of understanding. Like offspring from God's own self, He or She created spirits and the spirit world. This was created as an expression and as an extension of God's divine love. God genuinely loves his spirits, and spirits love God. Again I do not believe that God wants to be worshiped. God simply wants love in exchange for love.

God then created the universe and the planet earth as a large playground and school system for spirits. Spirit energy transforms into a soul and turns into a living organism to experience life. In order to truly embrace the human experience—and to learn and grow—the soul only remembers its current reality. This is why we forget about how we existed in spirit form. We do not remember what it was like in the spirit world. We are still connected to it, but we are disconnected just enough to be present in our current reality. Here on earth, we are completely focused on our mind, body, and soul, which creates our human experience

What then is the point of life? The purpose of life is simply to learn and to love. We become souls and take birth on planet Earth to learn and to continue expressing the love from which our spirits were created. The next obvious question is this: what are we here to learn, and is it in our control? Someone in passing once said to me, "We choose our own destiny before we come here." This really struck a chord with me. It also made a lot of sense in my spiritual journey.

The way I see it, when it comes to life, there are three things that are simultaneously at play:

1. YOUR PREDETERMINED DESTINY

Before we come to Earth we decide what we want to learn in this lifetime, and we plan out how exactly we want to achieve this. While we are in spirit form—existing in the spirit world—we sit down with God and our spirit guides and choose the type of life we wish to live, the parents we want to be born to, and the lessons we are eager to learn. We determine our kismet and our destiny while we are in spirit form. We write out many different options for ourselves, but the end result is usually the same.

This is why sometimes we experience déjà vu, get a gut feeling about certain things, and/or dream about something that later actually comes true. This is how some people just know that they are going to grow up to become doctors, or teachers, or famous actors. They know what their calling is in life. If they veer off into a different direction, they are not happy or fully satisfied.

We choose some of our friends and partners in advance also. We know them from the spirit world and already have strong bonds with them. This is why, when we first meet them here on earth, we are instantly attracted to them. This is why I believe that love at first sight is possible. This is why we get that unexplainable *I just know* feeling.

2. YOUR OWN FREE WILL

At birth we are given a clean slate. We do not remember what our pre-arranged destiny is. Our soul carries that information, and our intuition is set up to guide us throughout our journey. Even though we write our own destiny in advance, there is no one straight and narrow path to fulfill it. We have many options and many choices. We have the free will to alter, enhance, and even change some parts of our destiny—if we choose to. We can accomplish whatever we want in our lives. We are in control, and we can manifest the life that makes us happy. More than likely our choices and decisions will eventually align with our predetermined destiny, but we are not hostage to it.

Because we are here to learn, we write adversities for ourselves. Our free will determines how we act, react, and handle those adversities. If we do not learn the lesson that the struggle was supposed to teach us the first time, then we get another chance at it. If we continue to not learn the lessons we are predestined to learn, then the hardships may get more and more difficult and serious. However, it is still our free will to choose to either learn the lessons, or continue to ignore them.

Our mind, body, and soul are meant to work together harmoniously. Our soul is supposed to guide the thoughts and emotions that our mind creates; however, many people sever this relationship by disconnecting from their soul and by allowing their mind to function independently. As a consequence they stop hearing their soul's voice and are no longer guided by their predetermined destiny. Their free will determines whether or not they follow the journey they had written for themselves. God and the spirit world will not interfere; however, not staying the course definitely has its consequences.

In this situation people develop a false sense of intuition, which is guided by their mind rather than by their soul. They make choices and decisions which take them off their chosen path. They journey down a road that they had not originally intended for themselves. This leads to a lot of confusion, suffering, and heartache. This is why people feel lost. This is why some people struggle to determine what they are supposed to do in their lives.

It may hurt God and God's helpers to watch people struggle, but again they cannot interfere or override one's free will. This is also a part of the learning process. Many souls spend years not learning the lessons that they set out to learn. Instead they become bitter and resentful of their lives, and of the decisions that they have made. However, it is never too late; in a single moment, one has the potential to wake up, connect with his or her soul, and see what life has been trying to teach them all along. All is well that ends well.

3. OTHER PEOPLE'S FREE WILL

Connecting with one's soul and having a good sense of intuition is important. This helps us stay on course with our predetermined destiny and it guides our individual free will. However, we have to keep in mind that we are living on a planet with billions of people. Remember, God and God's helpers do not interfere with anyone's free will. Therefore, as you are exercising your free will, so is everyone else around you. Other people's free will impacts our lives almost as much as our own free will does. This is what makes life so interesting.

Before coming to earth, while we are still in the spirit world, we factor in other people's free will. We are aware of this; we are prepared for this, and we accept this. This is why we create various plans and scenarios for our life. In advance, we map out several different roads that can be taken upon our journey. The final destination is predetermined to be the same.

Sometimes other people's free will helps us, and it enhances our journey. Other times it may hinder us, and it may cause bumps in the road. We may come across some hardships and situations that we did not pre-plan, but we have to endure them as part of the world's process. These adversities are the hardest for us to cope with and to overcome because they were not predestined. People always say, "Life isn't fair," but I think life is fair. If someone's free will interferes in your life's path, then your spirit guides and angels make it up to you. Where one door closes, your angels and spirit guides create another door or window for you to open. Someone else's free will may cause you to detour on your life's journey, but you will find the original path once again.

You must not hold on to anger or resentment towards your life, towards yourself, and/or towards anyone else. After all, you don't know if a situation or a circumstance is predestined by your own spirit, is a consequence of your free will, or is a result of someone else's free will. This is what makes life so interesting. You never know why something happens or doesn't happen. You have to take life in strides, and see the lessons as they come before you. Have the courage and the strength to heal and to move forward. Life changes within an instant. Wonderful things are always around the corner.

Again the point of life is a school system and a playground. I believe this should be a 50/50 split. Learn 50% of the time, and have fun 50% of the time. So many of us spend the majority of our lives focusing on our struggles and problems. It is important to sort through your life and understand your lessons; however, don't forget to take advantage of the incredible playground that God has created for us. Have fun and enjoy yourself as often as possible. Make it a priority.

Thoughts. Ideas. Questions.

_____

_____

_____

_____

_____

_____

_____

CHAPTER 21: LIFE AFTER DEATH

As I have talked about before, fear comes from not knowing and from not understanding something. It is created from not being able to control something. Death is the greatest unknown that humans face in our universe. Personally, I have always been very afraid of death and its mystery. I was emotionally paralyzed by this fear. The very thought of death would send my heart racing. The most important thing I wanted to accomplish in my life was to reach God. I thought if I truly felt and experienced God, then I would somehow understand the purpose of death. I felt that I would no longer be scared or anxious about it; it would no longer be an unknown part of my reality.

I thought maybe after years of dedicated prayers and meditation—sometime in my old age—I might get a glimpse of God and I might understand the point of it all. Little did I know that it would happen in my early 30s, and it would be so simple and relatively easy. All I had to do was venture on a spiritual journey and then God—along with all my answers—presented themselves to me.

Before I talk about this further, there is one major element of our existence that I have to discuss. It can no longer be postponed. Now this may be a deal breaker for many of you who have been following and understanding my book thus far, but I pray that this is not the case. I hope by now you have gotten to know me a little bit, and agree with my logic and understanding.

This next concept has divided our world for centuries. Half of the world is going to fully agree with me—they already accept this as the truth. The other half of the world may feel like I dropped a bomb on them, because it completely goes against their belief system. I hope that you will continue to put your preconceived religious or non-religious thoughts and beliefs aside, and open yourself up to the possibility of gaining higher awareness. It is food for thought. Please do not discount what I am about to say until you have had a chance to read the rest of the book. I promise it will all come together and answer the profound questions of *What's the point of life, death, and the universe?*

I have already written in great detail about how our souls are old and wise. To recap, every living organism was originally created in spirit form and resided in the spirit world. Upon birth our energy transformed into a soul, which is connected to our mind and our body. The purpose of life is for the soul to learn, develop, and grow while expressing love. When we die, our soul's energy changes back into spirit form—once again we crossover to live as spirits in the spirit world. However, is it possible to learn everything in one lifetime? What happens if our free will doesn't allow us to learn the lessons we came to earth to learn? What if someone else's free will interferes with our learning process and our life is cut short? Would we never get another chance?

Why do we believe that this process can only happen once? If spirits only turn into souls once and experience life just once, then really what's the point? What would be the purpose of God creating this entire universe? Why would God send billions of souls to live here for such a short period of time? Why don't we just exist in spirit form for eternity?

I have been brought up in an Indian culture and the concept of reincarnation is something my religion strongly believes in. However, when I started my spiritual journey I put this belief aside. I wanted to see if my awareness and my soul searching would lead me to the same conclusion—and it has. Without a shadow of a doubt, I believe that our existence does not end when our heart stops beating. There is life after death.

Reincarnation exists. We have all had past lives, and our soul's journey does not end when we die. The mind, body, and soul make up our human experience. When we die only our body physically dies. Our mind and our soul exit the body and continue to live on. Like a movie camera, the mind records the entire life's experience and follows the soul into the spirit world. When the spirit is ready to take another adventure the mind and the soul will come back as another person. I think this makes so much sense. This is why some people claim to have past life memories.

The mind has an endless plethora of past life experiences recorded deep down inside of it.

We need multiple life times to learn, develop, and grow because one lifetime is simply not enough. Spirits start off young and innocent. With each lifetime our soul grows and gains wisdom. Throughout the soul's journey it becomes wiser, stronger, and more resilient.

I believe that each lifetime is spent serving different purposes. This is why different people focus on different things in their life. Think about it, what if every person in the world wanted to become an actor or an actress? What if no one wanted to go to school and become a doctor, a lawyer, or businessperson? How would the world function. Each person's predetermined destiny is divinely in tune with everyone else's. This is what makes the world go round. Some lifetimes are spent making mistakes and hiding from one's problems. Some lifetimes are spent working hard to learn difficult lessons. Some lifetimes are dedicated to helping and supporting others—while other lifetimes are spent mainly relaxing, having fun and recharging.

Earlier in this book, I spoke about the spirit not having a gender attached to it. A spirit is neither male nor female. You may be asking why then God created a man and a woman. I think the reason is that we learn different things as different sexes. We have all had lifetimes in which we were male and in which we were female. Some souls learn more as women, while other souls learn more as men.

When someone dies, either young or old, we are typically left asking *why*? *Why did they have to go, and why now*? *Why do people not live for hundreds of years*? *Why do some people die young and some old*? One of the biggest epiphanies I have had centers around this notion of why we have to die.

The word *death* is deeply related to the word *end*. Death equals the end of something. Instead of *end*, what if we correlate death with the word *leave*? I started thinking about the process of leaving. I realized that leaving is actually a monumental part of human life. When we find our self in a situation where we can no longer grow or learn, we typically leave.

People graduate and leave schools and universities because they have learned all they can learn, and they need to move forward. Sometimes in a job, people have learned all they can learn, they have developed as much as they can develop, and they are content with the experience they have had. They may reach a certain threshold that cannot be surpassed. In these situations people need to leave. They need to go elsewhere, so they can continue to grow. They may need a new job in order to feel fulfilled and challenged. This also happens in relationships and in marriages. People separate from others because they are no longer happy and unable to move forward in their relationship.

I believe this exact thing happens to our soul. When the mind, body, and soul combination is no longer capable of learning and growing, the soul subconsciously realizes that it is time to make a change. I believe this change is called death. In order for the soul to continue on its developmental journey, it has to die and change form. It needs to go back into spirit form and create the next phase of its journey.

The soul needs to leave its current situation and take on another brand new life—in a different body surrounded by different circumstances, different situations, and some different souls. This can happen to people at any age. We may feel like it wasn't someone's time to go, but we do not know what is happening inside of a person's soul. Some people stop growing and learning in their 30s, while other people don't even hit that threshold in their 90s.

Again, nothing in our existence is black or white. There are other scenarios in which people die. Since the purpose of life is to learn and to grow, we need the assistance of others to accomplish our goals. Sometimes people create soul-contracts with each other while they are in the spirit world. These contracts are prearranged and predestined. They are created to help others learn the lessons they wish to learn.

As hard as it is to believe, some souls predetermine to love one another, hurt and cheat one another, and even die an untimely death in order to help their loved ones and society learn lessons. No one consciously wants to die and leave this earth; however, as soon as a person passes away he or she is fully connected with his or her soul. Once they are back in the spirit world they remember the soul-contracts that they made before birth. I strongly believe that people who pass away are filled with love and understanding, not loss and sorrow like the people left behind.

In other situations, someone else's free will may cut another person's life short. Someone may choose to get drunk and get behind a wheel—thousands of people die in car accidents caused by drunk drivers every year. Someone may choose to pick up a weapon and end another person's life. I know this is so unfair, and we often blame God for allowing such things to happen. However, God cannot interfere in anyone's free will. Rest assured though, if someone's life is taken from them—before their time is up—God and the spirit world make it up to that soul, and to the souls that were forced to unjustly suffer the loss of their loved ones tenfold. Although it may not be any consolation in this lifetime, an abundance of extra happiness and success follows these souls into their future.

Again the twist is that you never really know which scenario causes a person to die:

1. A person can die because his or her soul is no longer capable of learning and growing in this lifetime.

2. A person may die a predetermined death in order to help their loved ones and/or society learn lessons.

3. Someone else's free will may cause a person's untimely death.

No one knows for sure why a person has died, and you do not know how or why you will die. Keep in mind some murders or deaths caused by some else's recklessness may be predestined by a soul-contract also. The point is that you don't know, and being angry, grief stricken for prolonged periods of times, and resentful does not help. It does not help the soul who has left, and it does not help you in your life's journey. The length of time that you spend grieving for a person does not represent how much you loved them. A deceased person can feel and experience your love in the afterlife, so focus your energy on loving them. Remember 98% of your soul already lives in the spirit world and is with everyone who has passed away.

Regardless of the situation or circumstance surrounding a person's death, death is inevitable. Yet as a society we fight so hard against it, and suffer so deeply when someone passes on to the next phase of their soul's journey. Someone once said to me when I was younger that, "One day you will be gone. Everyone you know will be gone, and everyone who ever knew you will be gone." I cannot tell you how many sleepless nights I spent being afraid of this reality.

It puts a smile on my face to know that this is not entirely true. Although our physical bodies die, our souls continue to live on. We may be separated from our loved ones here on earth, but our spirits are never separated. No one really dies. Some graduate and leave, some choose to quit early for the good of others, and some are forced to leave by others, but it is never the end of the road for anyone.

I always wondered what exactly happens when we die. Understanding and defining that moment is one of the major reasons I embarked on a spiritual journey. I believe that true death occurs the moment the mind and soul leaves the body. Sometimes this correlates with the exact time the heart stops beating and a person has taken his or her last breath, but not always.

Several years ago my grandfather, on my mother's side, passed away. He spent the last week or so of his life in the hospital extremely ill. The last two or three days he did not open his eyes and did not say a word. The doctor told us that they ran some tests that proved he was not responding to pain. This meant they were unable to do anything further for him. At the time we were angry that the hospital staff was giving up on him. We wanted them to try and do something to help him. Although we were in denial, deep down, we knew his end was near.

I remember one of my uncles saying that my grandfather is probably long gone. He said, "He's probably sitting with God right now meditating and singing hymns." I now understand that this very well could have been the case. His mind and his soul had left, and the body was just in the process of shutting down and taking its last breaths.

I believe when that moment of death occurs, we come into full awareness. We connect with our entire soul. We are reminded of the destiny we had written for ourselves, and recall the soul-contracts we had made with others. Every iota of stress, sadness, and anger leaves us. Worldly things no longer matter. Our spirit guides come down to receive us and bring us back home to the spirit world. We are once again completely surrounded by the divine white light of God. Love and pure joy greets us. A huge celebration commences in the spirit world, almost like a graduation party. Although we feel the suffering and the grief experienced by the people left behind on earth, we realize that we are not truly separated from them.

In the spirit world we then spend some time in processing mode. In this phase, the mind and the soul are connected in order to process the life that was left behind. The mind's function is to play back its recorded experiences from our life, and the soul's function is to determine what was and what was not learned from these experiences. The amount of time we spend in processing mode is determined by many factors. If we have done things that we are not proud of in our life, if our actions hurt or caused harm to other souls, or if we ventured far off of our predetermined destiny, then we may spend a lot longer processing and gauging our life. Our spirit guides and some designated angels help us through this phase. Once we are done processing, we choose whether we are ready to go back and take another shot at life, or choose to stay in spirit form.

Some people die and take another life fairly quickly. Some souls remain in spirit for a while—especially when ties to the physical world are holding them back. If they are concerned about guiding and protecting their loved ones here on earth, they may choose to stay in spirit form for a little longer. Spirits have the ability to come into the universe and check up on people from time to time. Diseased people often come to express their love and to reassure people. Unfortunately most people are unable to experience or communicate with them. This is because most people do not vibrate on a high enough frequency. Spirits also visit people in their dreams.

When people go to psychics to get readings done, or when mediums like John Edwards do their crossover sessions—where they communicate with spirits—they cannot control which loved ones come through. Someone may reach out to a medium and hope to speak to their mother or father, and instead a friend or a neighbor will appear in the reading. This got me thinking. If every single person who died is living in spirit form, then a medium would have the potential to communicate with anyone. I believe the reason one cannot control which spirits come through in a reading is because not everyone is accessible. Every person who has died does not live in the spirit world. Many spirits have transitioned back into souls and have taken another life. Psychics and mediums do not know which souls have moved on into another lifetime—and therefore are unreachable—and who is still present in the spirit world.

No one knows exactly how many lifetimes a soul has had, and there is no set number that has to be reached. A soul's journey takes as long as it needs to in order to learn all its lessons, and to develop as much as it can. I believe that souls who have grown to their maximum potential then become angels. Some angels eventually become spirit guides and archangels. This is the reason why spirit guides and angels understand us and our intent so well. At some point they have lived through our experiences. They were once souls who struggled, developed, and learned just like us. They have experienced every lesson that exists, and can empathize and understand what we go through in life.

Remember earlier in this book, I told you how I watched an episode of the Tyra Banks show which featured psychic children. I told you about one specific little girl whose gift was that she can see spirit guides. She told the audience that Tyra Banks had five spirit guides around her. She then told Tyra their names. Tyra was confused and joked that they didn't sound like black people's names. It seemed like she was trying to associate the names of her spirit guides with the names of her deceased family members.

The reason why she didn't recognize any names is because spirit guides are not people we know from this lifetime. Our spirit guides are not deceased family members or ancestors. Their relationship with us goes way back. They have been with us since the beginning of our soul's journey—from when we first transformed into a soul. They have been assigned to us for lifetimes and lifetimes, and they will continue to guide us for lifetimes to come.

Skeptics often ask, "If reincarnation exists, why is the human population increasing?" I believe that my spiritual journey has provided me with an answer to this age-old question. I will come back to this shortly.

Ideas. Thoughts. Questions.

_____

_____

_____

_____

_____

_____

_____

CHAPTER 22: OLD SOULS

On my spiritual path it seemed like the more answers I got, the more questions I had. After understanding all of the things above, I really struggled with one other thing. I could not stop thinking that if humans write their own destiny, then why would anyone predetermine bad things to happen to themselves. I understand that souls learn from adversities, but some people's lives are a lot harder than others. Why would people choose to be born into poverty or abuse? Why would some spirits agree to lose loved ones at a young age? Why would anyone write physical diseases or impairments for themselves?

As I mentioned before both of my parents were born and raised in India. My paternal grandfather was a Subedar in the Indian Army. My grandparents had four children of their own. They also adopted four of their nieces and nephews after their parents were killed, and they raised an orphan my grandfather brought home from the army. My dad is the youngest amongst the nine children. They were raised in a modest home, but always had an abundance of love, respect, and support. My grandparents did everything for their children. They taught them strong values, morals and emphasized education.

My dad and his older brother were only a year and half apart, and they were very close from a young age. They did everything together. They even got married two days apart from each other. In their early 20s they both decided to move to Canada. They dreamed of creating a better life for their wives and for their unborn children. My dad's passport and paperwork came in first, while my uncle was still waiting for his. My uncle convinced my dad to go ahead and leave for Canada. He planned to meet him there a few months later.

Unfortunately a few months after my dad left India, my uncle fell and injured his back. It didn't seem like a very serious injury at first, but the doctors suggested back surgery. During the surgery, the doctor accidentally pinched a nerve, which slowly caused my uncle to become paralyzed from the neck down. My aunt and uncle's dream of going to Canada was shattered, and, as newlyweds, their life turned a very different corner.

My uncle spent the next 30 years of his life incapacitated and paralyzed. He was incapable of having children, and only ever regained limited mobility in his left arm. Over the years, several of his siblings moved to Canada, and eventually his parents passed away. He was forced to rely on his wife for everything: from moving his body, to eating, to expelling his bodily waste. He led an incredibly difficult life. During the summer months the heat caused dozens of warts and open sores on his body, which caused tremendous pain. In the winters he would suffer from colds and pneumonia—India does not have heating systems built into homes.

My dad always fulfilled his duties as a son and as a brother. He bought his first home in Canada for $20,000 in the late 1970s, and when my uncle got very ill, he sold the house and sent money back to India. My dad must have taken over 15 trips back to India while we were growing up. None of them were vacations; he always went back to take care of his brother and to solve problems.

As a child, it was difficult for me to go to India and see my aunt and uncle in that situation. My siblings and I would do everything in our power to cheer them up. We would call them mom and dad, and we would call our parents aunt and uncle in front of them. This always put a smile on their faces.

Every time we went back to visit, it felt like their quality of life continuously deteriorated. To make matters worse, my aunt started having major problems with her eyes. About 25 years after my uncle became paralyzed, my aunt completely lost sight in both of her eyes. He was completely disabled, and the one person he relied on went blind.

I remember going to visit them after I got married, and my aunt was crying and saying, "I spent my life serving my disabled husband, and God rewarded me by taking away my eyes." It broke my heart to see the way they led their day-to-day lives. He served as her eyes, and she served as his legs. My uncle guided her actions by telling her where to go and what to watch out for; she would use her mobility to walk around and get things done. It is an unbelievable story. I probably wouldn't have believed it if it hadn't happened in my own family.

People often tried to explain their situation by saying things like, "It is God's will," or, "They both must have sinned in their past lives, and they are suffering the consequences in this lifetime." I personally could not fathom their suffering, or understand why this happened to them. My dad is a big jokester and a kid at heart; however, the older I got, the more I could see the pain and suffering my uncle's situation caused him. My dad would sometimes say things that gave me the impression that he felt guilty about his life and his situation in comparison to his brother's.

Eventually my aunt became emotionally depleted, bitter, and resentful of her life, which made it even more difficult for my uncle and my dad to help her. My uncle, however, always had a smile on his face and never gave up faith. He constantly prayed for a miracle, but sadly he never got one. He passed away in 2008.

My dad left for India as soon as he heard his brother was seriously ill again, but unfortunately he passed away before my dad even stepped onto the plane. I was pregnant with my son at the time and unable to travel—otherwise I would have certainly gone too. My dad spent nearly a month in India taking care of all the funeral and prayer services. He was also now responsible for my aunt. He had to ensure that she was properly taken care of.

While my dad was in India his back started hurting. By the time he got back to Canada he was in rough shape. His back progressively got worse and within a few weeks he was barely walking. My dad is extremely social and outgoing. To see him hunched over using a cane to walk was incredibly heartbreaking for everyone who knew him. I thought it was ironic that he went to his paralyzed brother's funeral and came back with this physical problem of his own.

Several months later a specialist told him that he had a few bulged discs, and he needed surgery. I went to that appointment with my dad, and when the doctor mentioned back surgery he completely froze. The irony just kept building—remember his brother became paralyzed due to back surgery. My strong, tall, fearless father was petrified of surgery. He didn't have to say the words, but I knew what he was thinking. I had to convince him that he was not going to suffer the same fate as his brother. We were in Canada and medical advancements have come a long way. He had tried everything and surgery was his last hope. He hesitantly agreed to the surgery and mentally prepared for it. Just two weeks before the surgery we all witnessed a miracle.

My husband and I had a party for our son in our home. There were a lot of people there, so I set up an extra folding table and some plastic chairs in our tiled kitchen area. After dinner, as my dad was about to get up, his chair slipped and he fell. His back first hit the chair end and then he hit the tiled floor. He was in incredible pain. Everyone thought that this fall might have made things worse for him. Surprisingly, a few days later he started to feel better. His back straightened out, and he was no longer in any pain. When we went to see the specialist, who was set to do the surgery in a few days, he cancelled the surgery! He said that in his 25-year career he has only cancelled two surgeries. He told my dad he had experienced a miracle.

My dad went back to being his active vibrant self in no time. My aunt passed away almost a year after my uncle's death, and my parents went back to India for her funeral and final arrangements. My dad's lifelong responsibility and obligations came to an end. His childhood home in India is now empty, but he took solace in the fact that his brother and sister-in-law were no longer suffering. Several months later my father was still grieving and trying to cope with everything that had happened.

After my own Reiki experience, which I talked about in Chapter 9, I asked that same woman—who is a healer, a medium, and is clairvoyant—to come to parents' house to do Reiki on them. I had told her that my dad says he has no pain, but I don't fully believe him. She knew nothing about my dad's back problems, his family, or his past. On the spot she thought about it and said, "He is lying. He still has a little pain in his back between his 3rd and 4th vertebrae." I was shocked because this is exactly where his bulging disc problem was. She then told me that his family members in the spirit world are standing at the door just waiting for her to go and see him.

This woman and I went to my parents' home a few days later. While she did my mom's Reiki session, my dad and I went downstairs and started talking. I told my dad about what she had said about his diseased family members waiting at the door to talk to him. I suggested maybe he should get a reading done. He had never done anything like this before, and he said he didn't want to bother the spirits. I thought if they are volunteering to come through then we are not bothering them, and perhaps we should hear what they have to say.

My dad and I then started talking about my uncle. I mentioned to him how I had heard that we write our own life and our destiny before we come to earth. This is a very different concept than the Indian belief of Karma, which is the belief that our present life is the consequence of good deeds or sins committed in previous lifetimes. However, neither of us could comprehend why my uncle would write a life filled with such heartache, physical pain, and suffering. It didn't seem possible that he could have chosen this for himself.

Anyhow, my dad agreed to let this woman do a reading for him before his Reiki session, and I sat in with him. As soon as this woman started channeling the spirit world, she said that she was inundated with voices congratulating my father and telling him, "good job!" She told him that his spirit guides are so proud of him, especially because he had never questioned God or his journey. He simply accepted things as they came and always kept his faith. They said they wished more souls could be like him.

My dad prays a lot and does an exceptional amount of social work. The woman told my dad that he had positively impacted a great many lives and had helped a great many souls on their journeys. I was so proud of my dad, but I wasn't the least bit surprised. He is an extraordinary man.

The woman then started to get glimpses of my dad's afterlife. She said after he dies there is going to be a large celebration in the spirit world. She looked at me and said, "You will be a mess, but the angels and God will be rejoicing at his return." She also told him that although he will be physically gone from this world, he will always have the potential to take care of his family.

As my father's reading continued, the woman started appearing confused. She said she was seeing cows, dogs, and animals and asked my dad if he ever lived on a farm. She said that the angels were showing her something like 200 pictures at once, and she didn't understand what she was seeing. She then mentioned that they kept showing her a blue door. It hit me and I quickly said, "India!" My dad's house in India had a blue door, and they are farmers. This is why she was having visions of animals. This woman has never been to India, and therefore could not understand what she was seeing.

She then started to cry heavily. She said that my dad's brother was there, and he wanted her to tell him to stop feeling guilty. My heart skipped a beat, but deep down inside I was hoping my uncle would come and help my dad relieve some of his emotional baggage. The woman went on to relay my uncle's message and spoke for a while. My uncle wanted his brother to know that he has nothing to feel guilty about. He said that being paralyzed or disabled was not my dad's path; my dad is living the life that was intended for him.

My uncle then said that he chose that life for himself because he wanted to learn patience. Had he not become paralyzed, he would have gotten caught up in material things and he would have wasted this lifetime. He said while he was alive he had forgotten his prearranged destiny, and that is why he always suffered and prayed to be healed. After his death, he remembered everything. He reassured my dad that he is okay and happy. The best part is that he learned the lesson that he intended to learn. He learned the true essence of patience, and he will never have to live another life like that again. He told my dad that he comes and sits with him while he prays. He said that they are not truly separated.

My dad and I were both astonished by the reading. This woman did not know that my dad had a brother, nor did she know anything about his past. She didn't understand why my dad felt guilty and for what. She said she was crying during the reading because she was feeling my uncle's emotions. It was only after she finished that we told her the story about how my uncle was paralyzed. I guess she has honed her intuition skills so much, and vibrated at such a high frequency, that she is able to communicate with spirits. We were unable to see them, but their messages were clear and on point.

During the Reiki session that followed the reading, the woman explained to my dad that the majority of his physical pain is caused by emotional pain. All the guilt and sadness my dad experienced when my uncle passed away latched onto his back and caused his discs to bulge. I can now tie this into the chapter I wrote about energy. Because my dad is a Trapped Energy type his unhealthy negative energy made him physically unhealthy. My uncle's life lessons were also meant to teach my father and us all some very valuable lessons.

Till this day I am shocked at how important lessons truly are. I am astounded that a soul would agree to put itself through so much in order to learn and grow. Perhaps my uncle had been trying to learn the lesson of patience in lifetimes before—in a more subtle and non-detrimental way—and failed to accomplish that goal. There is a reason why he took such drastic measures to learn his lessons, and it must mean a lot to the journey of his soul.

It took me a long time to grasp this and bring it into my awareness, but I think I get it. Because the spirit world does not exist in a realm defined by time and space, time is not an issue in that existence. In the spirit world a hundred human years can go by in a snap. Therefore our spirit is not concerned or afraid of spending time suffering or hurting in human form. The soul's main goal is to learn lessons that will help it grow.

When we are in spirit form, we are very powerful and can handle anything. A lifetime is just a drop in the bucket in the soul's journey, so we are more than eager to write challenges and adversities for ourselves in order to maximize our growth. The sacrifice is nothing in comparison to the reward.

When we become human and actually start living the hardships we chose, it is a whole different battle; we do not remember the strength, wisdom, and power that our spirit carries. We forget who we are deep down inside. We also end up getting wrapped up in material-comatose and often detach from our soul, which makes life a lot more difficult to understand.

Sometimes God and the spirit guides try to warn us not to take on too much, but we are sure we can handle it. People with the hardest lives, especially people who experience difficult childhoods, are the oldest souls. They are so old, so wise, and so powerful that they try to live out two or three lifetime's worth of lessons in one life. I think this is where the saying, "God doesn't give you anything you can't handle," comes from. However, technically speaking it's not God that gave us that struggle, we give it to ourselves because our spirit knows we can handle it.

Personally, I found this to be a beautiful realization. People with exceptionally difficult lives often spend time wallowing in self-pity and question, *Why me*? They feel as though God doesn't love them enough, or perhaps that the universe is punishing them for something. This realization should give people a much more positive outlook on their life.

I have shared this notion with many people who have led difficult lives. Hearing that they are old souls that are extremely powerful and wise, has given them tremendous solace and comfort. Initially, I thought that these people would not believe my theory, but surprisingly they quickly accepting it as the truth. When it was brought into their awareness, something deep down inside of them confirmed it as fact. This then allowed them to let go of some of the resentment and self-pity. It helped them find some of the strength and wisdom that their old soul carries.

Sometimes we take on too much in spirit form, and then life kicks our butt, so to speak. How many people do you know that have become bitter with their lives? No matter what anyone says to encourage them, they are unable to see the bright side of things. If you do not learn what you came to learn, and you do not do the work you set out to do, then unfortunately sometimes you have to come to try to learn it all over again in a different lifetime.

This is the exact thing that we want to avoid. This is why going on a spiritual journey, connecting with our souls, understanding the purpose of our reality, and having a conversation about it all is so important. We are here in our present reality and now is the time to heal, get inspired, and make the most of the life we have chosen for ourselves.

If we do not deal with our issues and confront our lives head-on, then we simply put them all into an imaginary suitcase and take them with us into the afterlife. We all have baggage we carry around from this life, and to top it off, most of us have baggage that we have carried in from previous lifetimes. We have unresolved issues and pent up emotions that we may have brought with us, and originally intended to sort through in this life. However, before we can get to that stuff, we need to make sure our slates are clear of issues created in this lifetime. Again, connecting with your soul, creating positive energy, increasing your vibrational level, and sorting through your life's lessons will all help you in the process.

Thoughts. Ideas. Questions?

_____

_____

_____

_____

_____

_____

CHAPTER 23: LESSONS LESSEN THE PAIN

No matter how we sugar coat it, life is difficult at times. There are count-less ups and downs. At times we experience tremendous joy, success, and fulfillment, while at other times, many situations and circumstances arise that cause us heartache, pain, and sorrow. Humans have almost become accustomed to a life filled with challenges and adversities. After a while, we do not even question them anymore. We do not think about the higher meaning; we do not see the bigger picture, and we certainly do not look for the lesson in everything.

Instead, our grief and suffering creates negative energy. Some people expel that negative energy onto others and out into the universe, and others keep it trapped inside of them and suffer alone. Some people choose to be in a state of denial and run from their problems, and others allow their problems to emotionally defeat and drain them.

Life is constantly changing. Before we get a chance to properly process what has happened, we have moved on to the next task or situation. Childhood problems carry into our adolescence, and the struggles faced during that time period follow us into our adulthood, and so on and so forth. There is a reason why so many people have a midlife crisis. Not fully dealing with forty or fifty years of pain, problems, and emotions is extremely challenging. Eventually it all starts to catch up to you.

Part of the lesson in life is trying to understand and determine lessons as they come. It is often more difficult for people to assess their own lives, and sometimes easier for other people to look from the outside and pinpoint the problem for them. This is perhaps why people turn to experts such as therapists, life coaches, and psychics. However, if you are not ready to fully open yourself up and bring your life's lessons into your awareness, you will not learn anything.

I have sat through countless discussions and therapy sessions where people have really opened up and spoken about their lives, their problems, and showcased their raw emotions. These people were desperate for guidance and were open to seeking assistance. While witnessing many back and forth conversations between individuals and experts, I started to see a pattern develop.

In these conversations, a moment almost always comes when the expert is able to lead the individual to the source of all their problems. They are able to pinpoint the one major problem that is holding them back in their life, and the lesson reveals itself. This is always such an incredible thing for me to observe. I am usually sitting to the side thinking, *That's it! That is the problem you have been struggling with. That is the lesson that you have not been learning.*

I typically leave the session feeling empowered, relieved, and excited for the person I had gone with. I am happy that they finally got answers, which they were so desperately seeking. Afterwards, the individual and I always sit down to discuss their revelations and epiphanies. Nearly 95% of the time they later say, "Well I really didn't get what the therapist was saying," or they say, "That was a waste of time, because the expert didn't know what he or she was talking about." Every time this absolutely shocks me. To me everything in the session was outlined in black and white. I know these people and their lives very well and usually agree with the therapist.

What was so obvious to the therapist—and to me as well—went completely over the individual's head. I started to realize that people are capable of evaluating and understanding their life's lessons, but only if they are truly ready to do so. It is not enough to one day wake up and say, "I am ready to face the problems that I may have been running from, and I am willing to see all the lessons that I neglected to see before."

If you prepare yourself, and do some work in advance, you will have a much easier time understanding yourself. Again part of the lesson is learning how to determine your life's lessons. Your friends, experts, and therapists cannot give you all the answers. They can only guide you in the right direction. Those answers have to come from within you. You have to accept them into your awareness, and you have to learn from them on your own.

I purposely saved this chapter and this discussion for the end portion of the book. In the introduction, I gave the analogy of an onion. I felt like I was trapped inside of an onion with layers and layers of truth and understanding around me, but no way of accessing them. I found it necessary to peel the layers one at a time from the inside out. I called this reverse peeling of an onion my spiritual journey. I needed to understand my life—the life that I have created—before I could understand the other realities that exist around me.

When it comes to truly understanding our life's lessons, I think it is essential for us to fully free ourselves from within our onion first. You need to venture on a spiritual journey and connect with your soul. You need to understand the universe and the spiritual world and ask for their guidance and support. You must examine and change your energy and vibrational frequency, and learn to surround yourself in white light. You need to step outside of yourself and see the bigger picture of life, death, and life after death. Once you have read and understood everything written in the pages that came before this, you are ready to once again return to your core and analyze your life's lessons.

You are now more open and aware. You will be able to see what you have been missing for so many years. You will no longer feel lost and confused when things are brought to your attention. I am certain you will see the lesson in everything that happens in your life. As a result, you only have to go through a particular hardship once. You will also be able to learn lessons from other people's lives and their experiences, so you don't have to go through it yourself. Lessons can lessen the pain and suffering you experience in your life.

I talked a little bit about my maternal grandfather in Chapter 20 and told you the story about when he was on his deathbed. My grandfather was a very educated, intelligent, and well respected man. He seldom spoke, but when he did everyone listened. Throughout his life he was incredibly independent and strong-willed. In his late 60s he suffered a stroke and it went undetected. Ever so slowly his health deteriorated and his body started to shut down.

A few years after his stroke, he had limited mobility in his legs and walked with a cane. However, he still drove himself around and took care of his own medical issues. He refused to accept assistance or empathy from others. He wouldn't even allow anyone to help him walk across an ice patch during the winter. Everyone wanted to help him, but it was important for him to keep his independence for as long as he could.

Soon he was unable to read, write, or drive. I remember he once told me that, for an educated person, his physical condition was worse than a prison sentence. He spent the last six years of his life completely bedridden and unable to speak clearly. He had no choice but to accept help from everyone around him. My grandmother and everyone did an amazing job taking care of him. Family and love always surrounded him. He passed away in 2004 just before his 80th birthday.

About a year ago, I decided to take a course to learn how to do Reiki. The woman I took the course from is a Reiki Master, and coincidentally she is also a clairvoyant and a medium. She says that she can see spirits and angels as clearly as she can see humans. I spent about eight hours taking her course, and she told me, early on in the day, that my grandfather's spirit was present in the room.

She said spirits typically only come into our sphere for a couple of minutes. They send their love and then they leave. However, my grandfather was there the entire time. He was making sure that I was learning everything properly. I wasn't really sure how I felt about that, so I didn't say anything in return. Every few hours I would ask her, "is my grandfather still here?" She would nod yes, and I wouldn't say anything else.

Near the end of the day, I felt like maybe I should ask him something because he was still there. Finally I asked my teacher, "Can you ask my grandfather if he is okay?" I wanted to make sure he was able to recover from being bedridden for so many years at the end of his life. She told me that my grandfather says he is just fine and incredibly happy. He then gave me insight into his life that I was not expecting.

He said that the lesson he wanted to learn in his lifetime was how to accept help from others. It took him his entire life, and the state of being completely bedridden, to actually be able to accept help from others. He had to be in that incapacitated state in order to learn his life's lesson. On the other hand, he said that the people taking care of him were meant to learn the lesson of helping someone without expecting anything in return. When you take care of someone who is disabled, there is nothing that person can do to return the favor.

I could not help but think that his life's lesson was so easy, and it saddened me that it took such drastic measures for him to finally learn it. This got me thinking about the lessons each one of us is trying to learn in our lives, and how much value these lessons hold in our soul's journey. How many people actually learn their lessons, and how many people die without ever realizing them? How grave and serious do things have to get before we take notice? How often do we bring a lesson into our awareness and truly accept the teachings that the lesson provided?

I firmly believe that disconnecting from your soul for the sake of material-comatose makes us neglect and avoid seeing what is directly in front of us. This only causes us more pain and suffering. Lessons can lessen the pain in our lives when they are confronted and accepted. However, if not learned, then life just keeps upping the ante.

As humans we are so persistent and determined. We can imagine how much more persistent our spirits must be. Before we are born, we write out our destiny and determine the lessons we want to learn in that specific lifetime with God and our spirit guides. We write adversities, situations, and circumstances that will teach us lessons. We advise our spirit guides to send more problems and challenges our way, if we do not learn the lesson the first time. This happens again and again and again. This is why so many people are stuck in vicious circles in their lives. They keep making the same mistakes over and over again. The consequences get more and more serious each time. We can only move forward when we finally face a problem, accept it, and learn from it.

Some of the lessons life could be trying to teach us are:
- Strength
- Sensitivity
- Perseverance
- Resiliency
- Patience
- Resisting temptation
- Gratitude
- Letting things go
- Ego management
- Compassion
- Humbleness
- Selflessness
- Confidence
- Understanding worldly possessions (having money, losing money, not having money)
- Accepting help from others
- Helping others without expecting anything in return
- Forgiveness (forgiving oneself is a lot harder lesson to learn than forgiving others

Our society is obsessed with dieting, losing weight, and looking good physically. Hundreds of millions of people struggle with their weight. Market data estimates that the weight loss industry is a 60 billion dollar industry in North America alone. Weight gain can be blamed on the fact that we live in a world of over excess. Many foods that we eat are fried, loaded with salt, and heavily processed.

I strongly believe that our physical body's condition is a reflection of our internal condition. Millions of people are emotional eaters; they try to fill the internal voids in their life with food. This is perhaps where the word *comfort food* comes from. When the mind and the soul are disconnected, the mind starts to follow the lead of the dysfunctional ego. The ego then forces one to keep their attention in the past or the future. This is how, in the present moment, one doesn't realize what he or she is doing. They may eat an entire days' worth of food in one sitting; thus, leading them to gain weight and perhaps eventually become obese. As I discussed in Chapter 6, living in the moment will help you connect with your soul and help you be aware of what you are eating.

Some people are emotional eaters who have internal problems, and there are millions of others who simply struggle with their weight due to the way their body is built. Weight gain is certainly a combination of both factors; however, I want to be clear about the distinction.

When I came to the realization that we predetermine our destiny and choose our own adversities, my attention almost instantly came to my physical body. I have never been obese or over-weight; however, I have a slow metabolism, I retain a lot of water, and I gain weight very easily. If I even look at pasta, I'll gain five pounds. When I was pregnant with my son, I gained 65 pounds, and it was such a tremendous struggle to lose the baby weight. I tried my best not to gain that much weight with this pregnancy, but I am well on my way to gaining the same amount. I already know that losing the weight for the second time is going to be extremely challenging.

While in spirit form, if we had the choice, why did most of us choose to struggle with our weight? When I thought about this, I was kicking myself for not choosing to be a person who eats what they want, hardly works out, yet never gains weight. Then I remembered that our soul is wise, and it is directly connected to God; therefore, it cannot steer us in a wrong direction to create unnecessary pain and struggle.

 While trying to lose my pregnancy weight after I had my son, I became very frustrated. I would see all these other pregnant women whose bodies bounced back in a few months, and I would get very down on myself. I felt sorry for myself and would often think, *I just want to be comfortable in my own skin.* After having this thought nearly a hundred times, I heard a voice in my head, which was certainly the voice of my soul…

the voice of God. It said to me, "Do you realize what you are saying? How would losing weight make you feel *comfortable* in your skin?" I had such an epiphany. Comfort doesn't come from how you look on the outside; being comfortable in your own skin means you're comfortable with yourself on the inside. Your internal comfort and happiness is reflected outwards, not the other way around.

Perhaps this was a lesson I needed to learn. Shortly after this realization the pounds started to fall off, and my internal healthiness started to match my external healthiness. There must be a lot of lessons that one learns from spending a lifetime controlling one's weight—lessons such as self-control, consistency, discipline, hard work, and determination.

Everything in life teaches us lessons; however, I believe that there is one serious emotion that is not related to any lesson. It serves no purpose in life or in our soul's journey: this emotion is guilt. Guilt is the most useless human emotion. I am going to say it again: guilt is the most useless human emotion! It is negative, it weighs us down, and there is nothing that can be learnt from it. Guilt kills the compassion we have for ourselves, and there is no end to the self-punishment that guilt creates.

I spent a lot of time thinking about this emotion and where it comes from. I think that guilt is created as a result of not understanding the true meaning of a lesson. Guilt masks the lessons. When we are unable to define or comprehend an emotion that is meant to teach us something, those feelings often default into guilt. Guilt is our generic default emotion. It has no logic behind it, and it is not rational; indeed, most of the times we do not even understand why we feel guilty.

Often others forgive us and move forward; however, the guilt lingers and continues to torment us for years and years. You need to focus on what is real in life. Guilt is not real. You must release yourself from underneath the burden of guilt. Only then can you see the true emotion that is hidden beneath, and only then will you be able to understand the lesson.

Before I end this chapter, I want to address a serious debate about reincarnation. Most non-believers say that reincarnation is not true because the population of the earth keeps increasing. I watched this debate on the Internet one day between lots of great minds. There was no clear answer for why the Earth's population keeps growing. I spent a lot of time trying to understand this, and it makes perfect sense to me now. First of all there is an uncountable number of spirits in the spirit world. Probably a number so large that us human's could never even fathom.

The reason why the population on Earth keeps increasing is because more and more soul's are not learning the lessons they came to Earth to learn. People are distracted; they allow their mind to take over by severing the tie between the mind and the soul; they use their free will to harm others and create negativity. They essentially waste their lifetime by wrapping themselves up in their ego. When these people die they are determined to go back and learn their predetermined lessons next time. Since the world's energy keeps shifting there are more and more negative factors, which keep people away from their spiritual path, so they likely have to take six or seven lifetimes to learn the lessons they intended to learn in one. More souls are coming back from the spirit world quickly, thus the population keeps increasing. The population is also increasing because many people are using their free will to not use birth control and by asking for many children.

I think as people are awakening and connecting with their souls, this will change the world's energy. People will start living authentic lives, which are in unison with their predetermined destiny. Souls will learn their lessons and slowly but surely, the world's population will start to decrease.

It's been a while since I have asked you to answer questions. I wanted to make some points clear before I asked you to reflect upon your life. Now is the perfect time. These are the most important questions you will answer so please take the time.

1. List three or four of the hardest things you have gone through in your life

2. List all the things that these hardships taught you

3. Has anything happened to you where you simply cannot understand and/or see the lesson in it? Recall that situation and write it down.

4. Yes or No. Are you carrying around emotions of guilt?
   If yes
   a. List all of the things that you feel guilty about.

   b. Yes or No. Do you agree that guilt was a default emotion
      you created because you couldn't understand the lesson in
      those situations?
   c. Write down what possible lessons you were meant to learn
      from those situations?

5. Yes or No. Do you feel like you are on your life's
   predetermined path?
   If yes
   a. What is your predetermined destiny?

   b. What are you meant to do in your life?

6. Do you feel like a young soul or an old soul?

CHAPTER 24: KARMA

Karma is an ancient belief system accepted by many religious philosophies such as Hinduism, Buddhism, Sikhism, and Jainism. It is the *cause and effect* theory that is determined by one's actions and deeds. To a certain extent, the notion of karma has been recognized and accepted worldwide. Westerners commonly associate karma with the concept of 'you reap what you sow.' If you do A then B will happen. Metaphorically speaking, if someone lights a fire that is meant to hurt someone else, and then they themselves get burned in that fire this is called karma or karmic justice—you deserve what you get based on your actions and deeds.

In Indian philosophy the concept of 'cause and effect' reaches out past one's life. It extends from one lifetime into another. The actions and deeds of a person cause consequences that one must face in the next lifetime; a person's karma follows them from lifetime to lifetime. Karma keeps people from committing sins and from hurting people; however, sometimes people's interpretation of karma keeps them from having compassion for others. If someone is underprivileged, ill, or has a difficult life, others view this as a result of their karma: they deserve their current situation because at some level they did something to cause it.

I strongly believe that our actions have consequences and the concept of karma is meant to teach us something; however, I cannot accept the fact that good and bad things happen in our lives simply because of the good and bad things we did in our past. The purpose of life cannot be to simply carry out cause and effect scenarios.

It makes so much more sense that the ups and downs in our lives are meant to teach us something. We choose our own destiny, and we write lessons for ourselves. A person is not born into abuse or poverty because they did bad things in their past lives. I believe they chose to be born into that situation because they are old souls, and they want to learn from being in that situation. My spiritual journey taught me that God does not judge our free will, and there is no such distinction between good and bad in the spirit world: everything represents different degrees of learning.

In a single lifetime our thoughts, emotions, and actions have consequences because they create both positive and negative energy. As I explained in Chapter 15, the energy we create affects us first and foremost. Our energy and aura impacts our lives on many levels. Karma is related to energy, but it is not exactly the same thing.

Our experiences from each lifetime are linked, and I do believe that the concept of karma holds an important key to understanding that connection. I spent a lot time thinking about karma and determining how it impacts our soul's journey.

Going back to the Law of Attraction, a lot of spiritual teachers and self-help experts say that our thoughts attract good and bad things from the universe. They state that our current life's situation is a result of our thoughts and actions. People who do good things, and focus their thoughts on those good things, attract more good things from the universe. If you do good deeds, more good will come to you.

However there are a lot of selfish greedy people, who are not very nice and positive in this world, who live in the lap of luxury. They are self-centered, they do good deeds simply for recognition, and they are always complaining. Although everyone has good qualities, these people seem to constantly create and expel drama and negative energy into the universe. Yet the universe continues to send them more good things: they gain more success, win lotteries, find love and become famous. Reality TV is filled with people like this. Clearly their positive thoughts, actions, and good deeds are not responsible for bringing them the money, success, and fame that they are enjoying. Have you ever wondered why and how this is possible?

On the contrary, millions of people are born into poverty, abuse, war and conflict in developing countries. The Law of Attraction cannot justify the horrible situations that millions of people live in. According to my theory and this book, human free will has caused such places to exist in the world, and people living in those circumstances have the potential to learn a lot of lessons; however, every single old soul cannot possibly choose to be born into impoverished war-stricken areas. Within my spiritual journey, I had to find an explanation for this, and this is where the concept of karma fits in.

I believe that deeds and actions work like currency that is depositing into a 'karmic bank account.' All the good, compassionate, selfless acts and deeds that we do creates positive energy. This positive energy helps us in this lifetime, and it also puts money into our 'karmic bank account.' This karmic bank follows us into the afterlife.

In the next lifetime, you are able to withdraw from this bank. The karmic currency buys you material goods, accessories, and worldly comforts that help you along your journey. Kind of like the rewards points your credit card company provides you. If you have a lot of points saved up, you can cash them in for free flights, hotel upgrades, or buy things with the points.

It is a little complicated, and it is not all black in white. One single scenario does not apply to every single person in the world. However, to a certain degree, we are all cashing in some of the good deeds we did in our past lives. The thing is, if we continue to withdraw from our karmic bank account and do not keep depositing into it, the bank account will eventually deplete.

If you keep reaping the rewards of your good karma by enjoying your worldly comforts and possessions, and you do not continue to do good deeds and actions in order to replace them, eventually your karmic bank account will be overdrawn. You will be left with nothing to take with you into the afterlife. If your karmic bank is empty, you may have a lot less to start off with in the next lifetime. Properly managing one's karmic bank account can also be a lesson that is learned throughout a soul's journey.

I also think that karma affects how we learn our life's lessons. If you are a positive person, who helps others and does good deeds, then your life's lessons have the potential to present themselves in a less detrimental manner. Your karma can soften the blows that life gives you. If your predetermined destiny was going to teach you a lesson through divorce, then perhaps your good karma can teach you the same lesson through a broken engagement. If a critical illness is written for you, then perhaps your good karma will turn that into a car accident or into a non-life-threatening injury. Perhaps you will learn a lesson through someone else's life experience rather than having to live it for yourself.

On the flip side your karma can make matters worse for you. If you are hurting other people, not doing good deeds, and if you feel superior to others, then you are creating bad karma. This can cause your destiny to become a lot more difficult. This is where the saying, "karma is a bitch" comes from. Bad karma can turn your destiny of winning a million dollar lottery into finding a penny on the floor. It can turn legal troubles into a prison sentence. You may have originally intended to learn a lesson from losing some money, and your bad karma can make it so that you learn that same lesson by going bankrupt or by becoming homeless.

This is why we have to be very careful about what we do in our lives, and how we view ourselves. If you are living a privileged life, instead of being self-centered and egotistical, feel blessed and give back. Doing good deeds does not mean attending charity events and showcasing how much money you donate to the world. There is, however, nothing wrong with attending charity functions and giving in that manner; however, one must pay it forward in ways that does not create any recognition.

There is a wonderful saying in Punjabi, which translates as, "If you donate something with your right hand, do it so discretely that your left hand does not even find out." The point is if you want to create good karma, keep doing good deeds from the bottom of your heart without expecting recognition or something in return. Keep making deposits into your karmic bank account. When you die, you do not take any of your worldly possessions with you. You do however take your karmic bank account with you into the afterlife. You may even see your good karma manifest in this lifetime as blessings in disguise.

CHAPTER 25: BLESSINGS IN DISGUISE

There is no such thing as a coincidence, and no such thing as luck. Everything happens for a reason and for your higher good. By *higher good* I mean things that serve your soul's purpose: the things that you came to earth to learn and experience. Things that serve your predetermined kismet and destiny are for your higher good.

Because prearranged destiny works in conjunction with free will and karma, life is constantly changing. Our intentions, our energy, and the tasks that we assign to our spirit guides all help orchestrate our day-to-day life. As much as we often hate change, life would be pretty boring if everything was predictable. Not knowing when something is going to happen and why is what makes life so exciting and interesting. The only constant is that everything happens for a reason.

What if the things that we view as bad in our lives are not necessarily bad? I believe that sometimes good things come in bad packages. Sometimes good things present themselves as a struggle, a failure, or as a loss. Like I said before, we should not judge the events or non-events in our lives as simply good or bad, because we cannot see the whole picture. Sometimes what seems like a punishment from the universe is actually a blessing in disguise: a blessing that is serving our higher good and our prearranged destiny.

I have had a string of bad luck in my career. I grew up with a low self-esteem, so I didn't have the courage to try modeling until I was in my early twenties. In the modeling industry, this is very old because you are competing with girls who have been working since they were 15 or 16. When I was 21, I got the courage to go to a modeling scout show. I was selected and even got chosen as a fitness model for a Miami based agency. I did a text shoot and had comp cards made; however, I never got a single phone call from the agency in two years—not one go-see, not one job.

I then got cast as the lead in a local Punjabi movie, which after months of filming fell apart and was never completed. A few months later Indian pop star Daler Mehndi, who at the time was at the peak of his career, came to Calgary. After a chance meeting, he asked me to be in his next music video. Needless to say I was ecstatic; however, no one from his group contacted me afterwards.

The following year he came to do another concert in Calgary. After being disappointed, I decided I was not going to go back stage or interview him for my TV show. Shockingly during the concert, he pointed me out of the audience and called me up to the stage. I was put on the spot, so I really had no choice but to go. Afterwards, I was escorted back stage, where Daler Mehndi apologized for not calling me last year. He told me that they were shooting a video in Chicago in a few months and he wanted to feature me in that for sure. He got me in touch with a few people who said they would contact me in two months. It seemed like such a done deal, that I even started sharing my good news with my close family and friends. Will you believe no one ever called me? They didn't even give me a courtesy call to say it wasn't going to happen.

After I won Miss Calgary I started modeling locally. Photographers constantly told me that I had potential, and that I should be doing this at a larger scale. After I won Miss Photogenic at the Miss Canada competition, I thought I had made it. If I had won Miss Photogenic at the Miss USA or Miss America pageant, I would have had tons of jobs lined up for me; however, things don't work that way in Canada. I did manage to get a Modeling contract with a reputable Toronto based Modeling Agency though.

With only a few months left till my wedding, I took a leap of faith and moved to Toronto to give my modeling career a fighting chance. I left my family, my friends, and my fiancé to see if I could make it. Unfortunately SARS, Sever Acute Respiratory Syndrome, reached Toronto a few weeks before I did. It was a deadly outbreak that was highly contagious. Toronto was devastated by this for several months. People were walking around with face masks, restaurants were empty, and millions of people were paranoid. Many film and music videos that were going to be shot in Toronto got cancelled altogether. In the three months I spent in Toronto I only booked a few jobs, I hardly went on any go sees, and I did not have any major auditions. Just my luck!

A few months after I got married, I got perhaps the best opportunity of my career. An Indian director, who I had met in Vancouver several years back, finally got budgeting and approval to make an Indo-Canadian film about AIDS. He told me that the lead role was already casted, but he'd like me to come to Vancouver to audition for the supporting role. After my audition, not only did I get a part in the movie, they gave me the lead role!

I played such an amazing character that goes from being a fun loving teenager to eventually getting aids from a cheating husband. There were so many extraordinary scenes that I had the opportunity of filming. In the climax my husband shoots himself, and they filmed my reaction. I literally hyperventilated in that scene. It took me 20 minutes to calm down after they called cut. I then had to repeat that in 10 different takes. I filmed a scene where I find out that I have aids, and the film ends with me dying while I'm singing to my five-year-old son. It was a very emotionally grueling process. Most nights I had to put cold presses on my eyes because I cried so much during filming.

I think because I had personally been in dark places of confusion and depression, it was easy for me to get into character. The entire crew really encouraged my acting ability. They repeatedly told me that I needed to go to Los Angeles and try to make it big. I enjoyed acting so much, and I dreamed about doing it for a living. I thought once the film is released, I would hopefully get some attention and perhaps a few more offers.

After a year of editing the film finally had a small premiere in Vancouver. Seeing the final project on the big screen was one of the most exciting days of my career. After the premiere, months and then years started to pass and the film was not released. No one had answers and they kept saying it will release soon. It has been over eight years, and the film never came out. I never even got a copy of it. The film producer has since passed away, so there is no chance that the movie will be released now. I don't understand how this could possibly happen, but I guess this is what they call show business.

In 2009 I eventually sold my entertainment company. After being on television every single week for over 13 years, I ended that chapter. I put the modeling and acting dreams away once and for all. Like they say, "We make plans and God laughs." A year later I was approached by a very big production company to discuss a possible national Bollywood television series. After months of interviews and auditions, I got the job.

I was still in the process of losing my pregnancy weight, and they informed me that in order for me to host the show, I needed to get back to my modeling weight, which I was gladly willing to do. I was so excited about this opportunity. I was writing, producing, and hosting an extremely high quality national series. I thought this is it. This is what I am meant to do with the next several years of my life. I started dieting and working out extremely hard. Thankfully the hosting portion of the show was not recorded until the end of the series production.

I wrote the shows; I travelled and interviewed many Bollywood stars and pop culture experts, and I watched an insane amount of movies. When we shot the host segments of the pilot episode, I was surprisingly not nervous at all. I stood behind the camera like it was second nature. I really felt at home and thought *this is what I am meant to do with my life.*

Less than a month before we were scheduled to record my hosting segments, I got devastating news. The network had gotten a well-known actress to host my show. Just like that, I was out and a she was in. I was still producing the show; however, I would not get the visible recognition as the show's host. I was humiliated. Everyone knew I was doing this show. I had to find the strength inside myself to tell people that I am no longer the host. The worst part for me was seeing all of the show's advertising say that the actress had travelled the globe to interview the Bollywood stars, when in actuality I did the interviews.

I started to think, *is this a cosmic joke?* At the time I was honestly upset with God. I had put my dreams of modeling and acting behind me. Why did God bring me this opportunity and awaken my dreams? The week the show aired I was quite upset, and I went to see my Reiki Master who always gives me great advice. She said to me that everything happens in life for a reason. She said, "Perhaps you are being taken out of certain situations because they will eventually hinder your growth." She also said that everything that I have learned will help me in the future somehow.

After this heartbreak, I picked myself back up and thought that there is a reason why my dreams were awoken. I had already lost a ton of weight, so I decided to give my acting career another go. I continued to lose weight; I got an acting agency and started to look for jobs. Since there is very little acting work in Calgary, I even started to think about relocating for a little while. I was doing all of this about six months ago. If you do the math, you can probably guess what happened to me next. I got pregnant! It took me three years to get pregnant with my son, and after two years of trying for a second child, I decided to focus on my career. In divine timing this is exactly when I get pregnant.

I am very lucky to have experienced so many amazing opportunities, regardless of the outcome. I now understand that some of my heartbreaks could have been a result of my free will, and the result of other people's free will. However, because there is a reoccurring theme in my life, I have to believe that all of my experiences will come in handy in my future. Perhaps angels intervened on my behalf and took me out of situations that would have hindered me from following my predetermined destiny. The actual experience was a blessing and being taken out of the experience was an even bigger blessing. I don't know for sure, but not knowing is what makes life interesting. I have already established that I would not have been able to write this book if I wasn't pregnant and at home right now.

For all you know, some of the worst things that have happened to you could have been a blessing. We are quick to write things off and label experiences as good or bad. We often get so upset and discouraged when things don't go our way. I am asking you to try to take a step back and accept things as they unfold without judgment, frustration, or dejection. Try to look at situations and circumstances that occur in your life from more than one perspective.

Most of us are in such a rush to get wherever we are going that the littlest hiccup along the way upsets us, ruins our day, and puts us in a foul mood. Getting pulled over by a police officer, being stuck in traffic, having a flat tire or turning back because you forgot something are all recipes for a disastrous day. However, have you ever considered the possibility that these roadblocks could have actually helped you or someone else in some way? Could it be possible that they actually caused you more good than harm?

Perhaps if you didn't get pulled over, then somewhere up the street you would have gotten into a car accident. Perhaps getting a flat tire prevented you from hitting a pedestrian crossing the street. Perhaps missing a flight, or having to cancel a trip saved you from something: this could have prevented you from getting ill during your travels, or maybe you dodged getting injured at your destination.

Billions and billions of people's paths and destinies are crossing 24 hours a day—so much is happening all at once. It is not happening randomly. God and the spirit world are divinely managing and orchestrating all that occurs. Sometimes our free will takes us on a path that is not quite right for us. Our choices and decisions may be conflicting with our intentions, and the things we are subconsciously writing on our chalkboard in the sky. As a consequence, sometimes we experience an angel intervention, and the spirit world intervenes on our behalf and sends us a blessing in disguise.

For example they may do something to help us escape a relationship that is draining our energy. They may create an injury or physical ailment in order to try and snap us out of a state of material-comatose. They may create a situation that prevents us from getting a particular job or promotion. They may pull us out of a situation that does not serve our higher good. In that moment we feel cheated, betrayed, and heartbroken, but in actuality the angel intervention was actually a blessing in disguise. We just can't see the whole picture.

I was watching Oprah Winfrey's biography in the show *Master Class*. She was talking about how she started off her career as a journalist who reported the evening news. The producers felt like her hair was causing problems for the green screen behind her, so they insisted she change her hairstyle. They sent her to a salon where the stylist gave her a French perm. After a few weeks her hair started falling out drastically.

Her hair was her pride and joy, and she was devastated when her damaged hair fell out in chunks. The channel had signed a one-year contract with Oprah, and now they didn't know what to do with her. They could not allow her to report the news looking the way she did, so they moved her to work on their local daytime talk show. Eventually she became the queen of talk shows and has become one of the most influential people in the world.

Watching her life's biography, all I could think about was that her devastating hair loss experience was actually a blessing in disguise. She always says that she would never have been happy reporting the news: it would have been a slow death for her, because it would not have provided her with the opportunity to teach. We now know that she was not meant to be a reporter; she was meant to be a talk show host. She was meant to create a platform from which she can teach and change the world, so her angels intervened and helped her fulfill her prearranged destiny.

Sometimes we want things in our lives and spend a lot of time and energy trying to achieve them. Often when we do not achieve those goals and/ or do not get what we want, we feel like failures. We feel like the universe is punishing us for something. However, perhaps those things do not serve our higher good and our predetermined destiny. Maybe not achieving something you desperately want is a lesson you intended to learn in this lifetime. This concept really got me thinking about miracles and why only some people get their prayers answered.

According to our souls, one lifetime is just a drop in the bucket in comparison to the soul's long journey. I think our soul is more than willing to face challenges and adversities, in order to gain the lessons it needs to grow and develop. Some of these adversities are exceptionally difficult for us to understand in our human form. For all we know some souls may have chosen to learn from having a critical illness, or from not being able to have biological children. God and spirit guides may have been given strict instructions to not help or intervene in those areas, no matter how much a person prays or focus' their intent on it. This may be why some people's prayers do not get answered.

I believe that people's prayers are answered when their wishes align with their prearranged destiny, or if serves their higher good. For example a person who is praying for a cure from an illness may witness a miracle because that illness was not originally in the plans for them. Other factors in life caused them to get ill. On the contrary, if someone wanted to learn from an illness and intended for others to learn from their struggle then they will not be cured. Again we cannot see the whole picture, and we do not remember our predetermined destiny. I am not saying that we bow down to adversities and accept defeat: absolutely not. We have to do everything in our power to fight, to pray, and to exhaust every possible avenue that can help us. Our prayers can be answered and we may experience miracles. However, if after trying everything your wish still does not come true, try to connect with your soul and change your perspective on it. Do not become dejected; do not become bitter; do not let this event change *who you are*.

There are so many broken, lost, and emotionally guarded people in this world because they have suffered through a loss or a failure that they cannot get over. They allow that incident to change who they are and what they have the potential to become in their life. A point has to come when you have to stop grieving, stop feeling sorry for yourself, and stop running away from the lesson that you were meant to learn. A point has to come when you surrender, accept it, and move forward.

I love the saying "it is what it is." There are so many things that you cannot control, and you certainly cannot change the past. You have no choice but to accept it, learn from it, and do your best to move forward. Open yourself up to the possibility that even though something hurt like crazy, it could have been a blessing in disguise. It could have been something that was meant to serve your soul's higher purpose. Your spiritual journey will help you connect with your predetermined destiny. This will allow you to see your blessings no matter how they present themselves.

Can you think of three or four incidences in your life that may have been blessings in disguise? Write them down in the space below.

_____

_____

_____

_____

_____

_____

_____

_____

_____

_____

_____

_____

CHAPTER 26: ONE SOUL FAMILY

The concept of soul mates is something that many people believe in. We have unexplainable connections with others. There are some people that are just meant to be in our lives. This connection and inner feeling often extends out to more than one person. I think that instead of a soul mate we each have a soul family: a group of people that we are related to on a spiritual level. People we have known from the spirit world, and in life-times before. One of the most beautiful realizations that I have ever had is that our connection to others extends even past the concept of individual soul-families. As a human race, we are all part of the same soul family.

We all come from the same divine creator. We are all connected by God's love, and God's light binds us all together. We all exist together in the spirit world as one big family. There is no race, gender, religion, social status or hierarchy, which differentiates our souls. We are all equal: one and the same. Even though we may not know each other now, we know each other from the spirit world. We have spent many lifetimes with each other in the past. Our relationships far exceed our human connection in the here and now.

Mankind has forgotten this reality. Sadly, the human race has found endless ways to differentiate and segregate ourselves from others. So many people have a 'me versus you' outlook. As a society we discriminate against each other; we judge each other; we put up walls and borders to separate ourselves from each other. Prejudices generalize and label people, cause conflicts, and foster hatred. We would not do this to members of our own family, so why is it okay for us to behave in this manner towards our global family?

When people in our own family make a mistake or go down the wrong path, we give them our empathy, our support, our guidance and our for-giveness. We pray for them and love them unconditionally. When people we don't know do similar things we become angry with them. We judge them, scorn them, and ridicule them.

Being livid at someone, discriminating against them, and deriding them only creates negative energy. When we hear about murders, gang violence, or terrorist attacks it has become our natural tendency to react with anger, and to curse and scorn the perpetrators. We wish ill upon them, and we want them to suffer and pay for their sins. There is nothing wrong with wanting justice in this world; however, our reaction to atrocities may be adding fuel to the fire.

As I have said before, I think that the world is plagued with conflict and violence because so many people have been expending mountains of negative energy into our world. Over time, and with each passing generation, the world's negative energy keeps multiplying and compounding. This negative energy is finding its way into billions of people's human energy fields. That negative energy entombs itself onto people's auras and then erodes their moral compasses. It fuels their negative emotions, intentions, and inclinations. Negative energy literally feeds the anger, resentment, injustice, conflict and violence in our world.

We need to realize that we are all one soul family, and we need to start treating each other this way. Each one of us is related to every criminal, wrongdoer, rebel, and extremist on a very deep, profound, and divine level. Similarly we are related to every saint, humanitarian, and good person in the world. Every inmate and every priest is equally connected to us. Each one of us has the power to support the causes of humanitarians and social workers, or we can choose to feed the cause of those creating conflict in our world. Each one of us is responsible for the energy we release into the world and for how that energy impacts our global society.

Love is the strongest energy in the world. If each person in this world sent love, guidance, and prayers to the wrongdoers of our world, we would create and expel exponential amounts of positive energy into the world. That positive energy is so powerful that it could rip the guns and weapons out of people's hands, so to speak. It could make people stop in their tracks, reassess their actions, and hold them to a higher moral standard. I believe that positive energy can bring peace on earth.

I was watching a television program on psychic investigations a few months ago, in which the police were using the assistance of a psychic to solve a murder: the program was based on a true story. The detective involved was skeptical, but his superiors suggested he discuss the case with someone who brings in a unique skill set. As the case proceeded the detective was highly impressed by the psychic's ability to know things about the case that the police had not even discovered. To make a long story short, the psychic was able to lead the police to identify the murderer. However because they could not collect solid evidence, they could not make an arrest.

Several months later that same murderer was brought into police custody for a small theft crime. When the psychic heard that the culprit was behind bars, he prayed and sent the murderer love, light, and compassion. The same night the convict started screaming in his jail cell confessing to murdering a woman several months back. No one had to force the truth out of him, no one had to build a case against him, and no one had to fight for justice. The positive energy the psychic sent him made him repent his actions all on his own.

If one person has this much power over another individual, imagine the power and influence millions of people could have on drug rings, terrorist cells, and organized crime? If we all work together to send them positive energy, we could stop them. Don't forget that the positive energy you create impacts you, your life, and your surroundings first and foremost. It is a win-win situation that is so simple and so easy. Create feelings, emotions, and actions that showcase the love and compassion you have for yourself, extend that love and compassion out to your loved ones, and then maintain a similar attitude towards your entire soul family— the world.

Because we are one soul family, and because the majority of our souls exist outside of our body in the spirit world, we have this ability to connect with each other on a much higher level. Through our thoughts, intentions, and our spirit guides, we have the ability to communicate and influence each other non-verbally. Our energy and our vibrations are constantly communicating with those around us, and our souls are constantly sending us information about each other through our intuition. This isn't a special skill that only some people have; every single person has this ability.

A couple of years ago, my two girlfriends and I went out to grab a bite to eat. We went to a busy pub that had live entertainment. One friend was sitting beside me in a booth and one friend was sitting across from us. I had known the woman sitting beside me for many years. She was a close friend who shared and discussed everything with me. We'd had countless intimate conversations, and I thought I knew everything about her life.

On that particular night we were chatting like usual when all of a sudden I had an overwhelming feeling; it felt like someone had hit me in the head with a thought. Without even thinking about it, I looked at my friend sitting beside me and said, "Did something happen to you when you were a child?" I didn't know where that came from, but I could not stop the words from coming out of my mouth. She went completely pale and said, "No, what do you mean?"

It was completely not the right time or place to have a serious conversation. The restaurant was completely full, it was loud, and our other friend was sitting across the table from us, but I just could not let it go. I said to her, "Seriously, something happened to you when you were younger; tell me what happened?" She broke down and started crying, and she said she didn't want to talk about it.

Normally I am very respectful of people's privacy and would never push anyone to talk about something they didn't feel comfortable discussing; however, something inside of me told me that she really needed to get something off her chest, and if she doesn't do it now it may never happen. My other friend and I comforted her a little and then she finally broke her silence and told us that she was seriously molested when she was a child, and she has never told a single person. This confession opened up the door for our other friend to share something traumatic that happened to her. Right there in that incredibly loud busy restaurant the three of us had an incredible life altering therapy session.

As I was driving my friend home, my mind was replaying the events of that evening. I apologized for having pushed her. I told her how this strange feeling came over me that she was hiding something about her childhood; it was something that had never occurred to me before. It really caught me by surprise and I didn't know where it came from. She then said something that shook me to my very core.

She said that as we were sitting there having small talk, she was actually thinking about the molestation in her mind. She was thinking, *I need to tell someone, but how am I ever going to bring it up*? She told me that as soon as that thought crossed her mind, I started questioning her about her childhood. She was thankful for it because she had been drowning under the burden of that secret her entire life, and had I not pushed her, she would never have told anyone. We both paused and then with wide eyes we looked at each other with the exact same thought. I said, "I read your mind?" She responded, "You read my mind!"

I was so happy and relieved that she was able to release her emotions; however, the incident really freaked me out for a while. I questioned how it was possible that I could have read someone's mind, but that was the only explanation for it. Since then similar situations have happened to me, where I feel like my intuition is telling me something about someone else. I have been able to control it a little bit and usually will wait until I am alone with that person to ask them about it.

Over time I have realized that this is not a special gift or psychic ability that I possess. These types of situations are possible because we are all one soul family and our souls communicate with each other in many ways. We reach out to one another for support and guidance, even if we do not express it verbally. I'm sure that my spiritual journey has helped me connect with my soul and has increased my intuition and vibrational frequency. Every single one of us has this ability to communicate with each other on a spiritual level. I started to think that if people can subconsciously reach out to us in this manner, then we can do the same thing.

So many of us hold pent up emotions inside of ourselves as a result of something that someone else has said or done. Often other people's free will prevents us from getting closure on certain situations. We may not have found a way to contact them, they may refuse to talk to us, or we may not have the courage to speak to them directly. That person may have passed away, or they may be incapable of accepting responsibility for hurting you. As a result that person remains in our psyche—in our mind and in our thoughts. No matter how hard we try, we cannot forgive or forget.

Because only roughly 2% of a person's soul resides inside his or her body, and the remainder exists outside in the spirit world, you have the ability to communicate with 98% of any person's soul at any given moment. Because we are all one soul family and are connected on an incredibly high level, you can release someone from your psyche without having physical contact with them. Our thoughts, intentions, and spirit guides can help us talk to anyone, and can relay our messages to them. By closing your eyes, wrapping yourself in white light, and focusing on another person you can bring them into your sphere on a soul level. You can say whatever is on your mind, and tell them whatever you want. Trust me they will hear you.

Your psyche should only be reserved for your soul, your spirit guides, and for God. If you allow anyone or anything to linger in your personal spiritual space for a prolonged period of time, it will impact your life on many levels. It will develop a slew of feelings and emotions that create negative energy. This negative energy will attach itself onto your aura, and eventually lower your vibrational frequency. Your lowered vibrational frequency may prevent your spirit guides and angels from guiding and supporting you through your life. Because everything is connected, everything has a domino effect.

When people pass away we often have regrets and guilt about the things that we should have said or should not have said to that person. Remember, guilt is the most useless human emotion in the world, and we learn and accomplish nothing from it. You no longer have to feel like you lost your chance to communicate with those who have passed away; you can call any deceased person into your sphere and talk directly to their soul. Chances are they have already read your intentions and know how you are feeling, but expressing it will help you.

So take some time to assess and evaluate who or what remains in your spiritual space. Release them from your psyche by having a conversation with that person and expressing whatever it is that you are holding onto. Releasing someone from your spiritual space does not mean that you stop loving them, or that you want to forget them. It's about freeing yourself and moving forward. Write down your thoughts on the space below:

_____

_____

_____

_____

_____

_____

_____

_____

_____

_____

CHAPTER 28: FIND YOUR FUEL

It is my sincerest hope that this book has led you on a spiritual journey. I hope it has taught you something that will help you better your life. Instead of saying *better your life* I should say it would better your life's experience. At the end of the day, your perception and your outlook only decipher a good or bad life.

According to one's soul a good life is one that is filled with growth, development, and lessons learned. It's not about avoiding conflicts and dodging adversities; it is about persevering and staying positive even during difficult times. One should be like a strong tree that is deeply rooted into the ground. Come rain, wind, sunshine or storm the tree's branches are flexible and go with the flow; however its trunk and its roots remain solid; they are resilient and do not waver in the least. Even if a branch gets ripped off and destroyed, the tree has the strength and the determination to grow it back once again. This is how we should all be in our lives.

As I said in the beginning, spirituality and awareness cannot be taught. They can only be inspired and awoken. However, I do understand that we often need guidance and direction. We are strategic and orderly human beings that learn from logic and explanation. I hope that I have provided that in this book.

We each need to find our fuel in life. We need to find our purpose, and find out what drives us to reach our potential. I love the saying, "it's all about the journey, not about the destination." All we have is right here and right now. It is the present moment that matters. Every mistake, every hardship, every up and down experienced in our lives has helped us get to this exact moment. It has prepared us for our present situation and for our future. Not a second of our life was a waste. It all happened for a divine reason.

I do not believe that there is one single thing that defines our purpose in life. We are meant to do and experience many things. However, there may be one common thing that helps us fuel our life. That fuel we must find. So let's recap all the steps that one can take to find their fuel:

1. First and foremost make the decision to embark on a spiritual journey of your own. Make the choice and take out the time.

2. Let go of all your preconceived beliefs and ideas. They will only stand in your way. Put your religious and non-religious beliefs on the shelf for a little while so you can develop your own intuition.

3. Understand the relationship you have with your mind and your soul. You need to spend time silencing your mind, so you can hear your soul.

4. You need to take yourself out of a state of *material-comatose* and start actively participating in everything that you do.

5. Who I am and what I do is not the same thing. Who you are is not the same thing as what you do. In order to find out *who you are,* you need to let go of who you think you are. Give up everything you think you know about yourself.

6. Who you are comes from your soul, not from your mind. You will soon realize who you are when you start connecting with your soul.

7. In order to connect with your soul and figure out who you are you need to:
    a. Take yourself out of autopilot
    b. Live in the moment
    c. Stop reading and reacting

      d. Empower your soul

      e. Sharpen your intuition

8. Find your worth by realizing that you are a direct extension of God, and you are worthy of every single thing in your life.

9. Before you can express anything externally, you have to whole-heartedly feel it internally. Before you can love anyone else, you have to first love yourself. Before you can make someone else happy, you need to make yourself happy. Before you can heal the world, you have to heal yourself. Once you have experienced love, happiness, gratitude, and forgiveness inside yourself, you can then project it outwards onto your loved ones and out into the world.

10. Spirituality is not something you practice, it is a major component of who you already are. In order to live a meaningful life, you need to spend time creating an internal relationship with yourself.

11. Start to be conscious of your free will. Determine how you have been exercising your free will thus far. How can you change it to better your life and to better impact the world?

12. Spend some time reflecting on your relationship with God. Are you, or have you been, upset with God? Do you blame God for problems in your life? How do you communicate with God? What are you communicating? What do you want God to know?

13. Become a grateful person. Gratitude is another word for love. God does not want to be worshiped; He or She simply wants love in exchange for love. When you are grateful you are expressing love. Write down all the things that you are grateful for. Start with your heartbeat and work your way out.

14. One of the best problem solvers to have ever lived is Albert Einstein. He famously said, "We can't solve problems by using the same kind of thinking we used when we created them." Make a list of what you perceive as the problems in your life. Change the way you think and see if you can find a solution to these problems. The answers will come from within.

15. Start to recognize that you attract things to your life based on your intentions. Thoughts are random, but what you intend those thoughts to mean is not. Your intentions, whether they are positive or negative, bring you more of the same. Start creating positive intentions around the things you want. Intend to have good health and meet great new people. Intend to have abundance and attract big things to your life. I love the saying, "You get in life, what you have the courage to ask for"

16. Create a *chalkboard in the sky* and write your intentions on it. Think of ways you can make your intentions come true by assigning detailed individual tasks to your spirit team. If you want a house, put that on your chalkboard. Assign it as a task to one of your spirit guides. Then imagine in detail what every nook and cranny of the house will look like. If you want a new man in your life, list what traits you want that man to have.

17. By understanding what I call the *energy equilibrium*, determine if you are creating positive energy or negative energy. Determine how this energy is impacting your life and how other people's energy is impacting your life.

18. Identify your energy type as either a *Roller Coaster Energy, Go-To Energy*, or as *Trapped Energy*.

19. Identify who or what things you are carrying around in your sphere as baggage. After processing the situation and how it made

you feel, release anyone or anything that is holding you back from moving forward in your life. Stop living in the past because it no longer exists and it no longer serves you.

20. Never yell, scream, or fight with others. Never engage in situations which create negative energy. Walk away and do not participate. When everyone has calmed down, come back and deal with the situation.

21. Small amounts of positive energy can combust mounds of negative energy. Love is the strongest energy in the world. Through loving intentions, laughter, affection, and charity work you can create tons of positive energy every day. This positive energy will significantly improve every aspect of your life. After passing through your aura, the positive energy will also help neutralize the immeasurable amounts of negative energy, which currently has a strong hold on our world.

22. Everyday wrap yourself in white light and use it as an armor of protection. Spin the white light out to protect your loved ones. Then take the white light and wrap the entire globe with it. If we all start doing this, we will see incredible change in our world's energy.

23. Think about your karmic bank account, and think about what you are depositing and withdrawing from it.

24. Go through the answers you have written down in this book and reflect on your journey. Are there some answers you could not answer before, but can answer now? Are there some answers you would now change?

25. List all the things that you feel guilty about in your life? Remember guilt is the most useless emotion in the world. There

is nothing to learn from guilt. It is simply a default emotion
that manifests from not knowing the true lesson of something.
Identify the guilt, let it go, and then try to find the true lesson
behind that situation.

26.   Think about the other lessons you have learned thus far in your
      life. More importantly think about the lessons that life has been
      trying to teach you, but you have not learned. Never run from
      your problems or avoid what life is trying to teach you.

27.   I believe the smartest people in the world are the ones who listen
      to other people. Listening gives you the opportunity to learn from
      other people's mistakes. Take the time to genuinely talk to others.
      Listen to their problems and learn from their lessons, so you don't
      have to live through them yourself.

28.   Before we are born, we sit down with God and our angels and
      determine what we want to do in this life. We decide who our
      parents are and we create soul contracts with certain people. We
      write out the hardships we want to go through and the lessons we
      want to learn. We create several paths, but the end destination is
      the same. Are you on your life's predetermined path, or is there
      a nagging feeling that is telling you that you have diverted from
      your original plan?

29.   All of this reflecting should give you some insight into what you
      want to do with your life. Find whatever it is and use it to fuel your
      life. You don't need to be like anyone else. Be the best you that
      you can possibly be, and then improve on it every day. Don't be
      hard on yourself. Relax and enjoy every day.

30.   Don't judge the events or non-events in your life as merely good
      or bad. Remember you cannot see the entire picture. Someone
      may wrong you because of a soul contract you created with him or

her in the spirit world. That person may have agreed to hurt you in order for you to learn a lesson—an important lesson you came to earth to learn. However, your own free will and decisions can harm you. There will be times when someone else's free will can get in your way, and let's not forget that your karma can also come back to bite you in your behind. The point is you never know why things happen or don't happen. This is what keep's life so interesting. This is what makes life so amazing. Don't spend time focusing on why things happen. Take every day in stride and don't worry about it so much. Just live.

31. Be selfish because you have to look after yourself first and foremost. However once you have spent some time doing this, don't continue to be selfish. *Pay it forward.* Use your intentions, your energy, and your angels to help heal our global society, Mother Nature, and our universe. You are here to change the world. You have the power to make this world a better place for everyone.

32. Because one creator created all that exists, we are all equal. We are all one in the same and part of the same soul family. You are equally related to every priest and every inmate in this world. Like your own family members, treat everyone with compassion and forgiveness. Instead of being judgmental and resentful towards the wrong doers in our society, send them love and compassion. Prey for those who have gone down dark paths. Don't feed their anger with your anger.

33. Remember God created this earth as a school system and as a playground. Don't spend your life simply focusing on the schooling aspect of life. It should be a 50/50 split. Spend 50% of your time focusing on life's lessons and working on your internal life. Spend the other 50% of your life having fun and enjoying the incredible playground God has created for us.

When it comes to God and spirituality, no one can provide any concrete evidence. There is no scientific proof. However, we are all intelligent enough to recognize that there are things outside the scope of science that impact our lives. My spiritual journey, my awareness, and my intuition told me everything that I have said in this book. With every fiber of my being, I believe them to be true. I know that I have found answers to the profound question of, *what's the point?* This is what resonates within me as to what the point is of life, death, and the universe is.

Writing this book has been an entirely new phase of my spiritual journey. In the introduction I had mentioned that it is important to reflect on our past. Events and experiences leave cuts and wounds in our life's story. By revisiting former heartaches and heartbreaks, we are able to heal old wounds and finally put the past to rest and move forward. Writing anecdotes about my life gave me the opportunity to focus on my past. I found wounds and gashes that I didn't even know existed. I have had countless realizations and epiphanies as I was writing. I have written entire chapters without being fully conscious of what I was writing. Afterwards when I went back and read what I had written I thought, *Where did that come from? How did I know that?* I simply allowed my soul's voice to pour onto these pages. It is from my heart to your heart: from my soul to your soul.

I only want you to believe me or agree with me if your own intuition and inner voice allows you to. This book is meant to provide food for thought. It is meant to expand on a discussion that only some people are having in our world. I have not stopped learning, and I am excited to see how much I can learn from the conversations that will follow this. Please visit www.gurdeepbrar.com and tell me about your journey. I sincerely hope you were able to heal some of your old wounds. I sincerely hope that you are now ready to move forward and take charge of your life.

It is due time that we communicate with each other and inspire each other to become better individuals. It is due time that we recognize and share each other's pain and confusion, and provide support and direction. It is due time that we stop the suffering that exists in our world and start the healing process. One person at a time, we can bring love, understanding, and awareness into our own lives and then project it out into the world. We can achieve peace on earth and happiness for all. Happily-ever-after is no longer only meant for fairytales.

References

Daniel Akst, Temptation: Finding Self-Control in an Age of Excess (New York: Penguin Books 2011)

Sophy Burnham, *The Art of Intuition: Cultivating Your Inner Wisdom* (New York: Tarcher 2011)

Rhonda Byrne, *the Secret* (New York: Atria Books 2006)

Deepak Chopra, *Reinventing the Body, Resurrecting the Soul: How to Create a New You* (New York: Harmony Books 2009)

Wayne W. Dyer, *There's a Spiritual Solution to Every Problem* (Kent UK: Quill 2003)

Brenda Shoshanna, *Fearless: The 7 Principles of Peace of Mind* (New York: Sterling Ethos 2010)

Diane Stein, *Essential Reiki: A Complete Guide To An Ancient Healing Art* (New York: Crossing Press 1995)

Eckhart Tolle, *The Power of Now: A Guide to Spiritual Enlightenment* (Novato, California: New World Library 1999)

Neale Donald Walsch, Conversations with God: An Uncommon Dialgue (Book 1) (New York: G.P. Putnam's Sons 1996)

John White and Stanley Krippner, Future Science: Life energies and the physics of paranormal phenomena (New York: Anchor Books 1997)

About the Author

Gurdeep Brar was born and raised in Canada to immigrant parents who came to Canada to provide a great life for their children. Externally she was an actress and a model who had tremendous pageant success. In 1996 she was 1st runner-up Miss India Canada. She was one of the first visible minorities to win Miss Calgary in 2001. She went on to become 1st runner-up Miss Canada and was Top Model Canada 2002. She also ran her own local entertainment company called Sabrang Enterprises Ltd and spent over ten years working on television and radio.

Internally, however, she was lost, depressed, and self-deprecating. After years of feeling unworthy, she embarked on a spiritual journey, which provided her with countless realizations and revelations. Brar opens up her life and her heart to the world by sharing her personal story and spiritual reflections. Aside from writing, Brar is a Reiki Master, a Motivational Speaker and a Life Coach. She is also a proud mother, who in fact wrote this book while she was pregnant with her second child.